Emotional Healing
with Essential Oils
A journey of self discovery

Trish Nash

Emotional Healing With Essential Oils © Trish Nash

Disclaimer

This book is not intended as a substitute for medical advice. The information contained herein should not be used to treat, diagnose, or prevent a medical condition without the advice of an appropriate qualified health professional. The reader should consult a physician in matters relating to his or her personal health and wellbeing; particularly in regards to any symptoms that may require diagnosis or medical attention. The author does not assume any responsibility or liability for errors, omissions, contrary interpretation of this information, and any damages or costs incurred through actions taken due to information in this text.

National Library of Australia Cataloguing-in-Publication entry:

Creator: Nash, Trish, author.

Title: Emotional Healing With Essential Oils / Trish Nash.

ISBN: 9781925497533 (paperback)
                  9781925497595 (eBook)

Subjects: Self-actualization (Psychology)
                  Essences and essential oils--Therapeutic use.

Dewey Number: 158.1

Published by **Trish Nash** and InHouse Publishing
www.inhousepublishing.com.au

To my amazing son Alex
for all your support and encouragement

THE
essential
KN◯WLEDGE
── SERIES ──

Would you like to utilise this material to educate others about emotional healing? We have collaborated with Essential Oil Supplies Ltd to bring you a selection of complimentary educational material as part of their Essential Oil Knowledge Series. To preview and purchase them visit www.essentialoilsupplies.co.uk

Contents

CHAPTER 1

New Beginnings

Life is all about our own individual journey. Where we are going, our experiences, perception and where we have been. I am offering a road map to help navigate the rocky road of life and progress in your emotional healing. You may ask yourself, Where do I start? One step at a time. Like anything, change takes time and it becomes easier as you break old, negative habits and create new, positive ones in your life. You are already spending energy and time on repeating the negative thought patterns in your life. Why not replace the negative thoughts with positive ones that have the power to change your life from negative to positive?

Start by getting back to the basics of what's really important to you and what makes you happy. Knowing what you want out of life sets clear goals, helping you embrace your journey of self-discovery and emotional healing. By discovering who you truly are, you will release old scripts and belief systems that no longer serve your true self. It starts with clearing your mind and looking at patterns from a new, positive perspective. Also, when we take care of our physical body, we have the resources, clarity and energy to accomplish our goals. There is no quick fix and it does require repeated action on your part. Think of your brain muscle in the same way as your bicep muscle. When you do arm curls day after day, your muscle becomes lean, strong and toned but when you stop it gets saggy and weak. The same concept is true with your thought patterns. If you train your brain on a daily basis through meditation, constructive life scripts, positive attitude, affirmations, journaling, maintaining balance, filling your tank, etc. it will become stronger and more focused on the life you want, not the life you don't want.

At a primal level, we all want to be loved and belong to a community. Deep down, everyone wants to feel love and joy. The need to be a part of a community is in our genetic makeup and was very useful for our ancestors' survival. Try viewing the world with eyes of love; it will open your heart to compassion, forgiveness and empathy. Even the most horrific person wants these things, often they just don't have the skills or knowledge to achieve the desired results. Instead we are driven by learned behaviour patterns—twisted concepts of love, power and control—to meet these unfulfilled needs. The outcome, of course, is misery, isolation, fear and hatred. Through ignorance, the pattern continues for generation after generation as it becomes the normal state of living.

How do we humans store and process emotion information? It was once believed that the brain was the only place we process and store emotions. In reality, we have three main emotional centres: the brain, heart and stomach. Current research shows there are more neuro-connections going from the stomach to the brain than the other way around. Are you surprised? Think of it in terms of your own experiences. The anxiety felt in the pit of the stomach—that gut feeling. The heart literally aching in pain or feeling as if it has been ripped out of your chest. These are emotional responses to situations in your life playing out in that area of the body. We can also store emotions in any part of our bodies. This can manifest throughout the body with aches and pains to serious disease, even death. It's your body's way of saying, 'Hello, is anybody out there?' It's like a warning light on the dashboard of a car. When the light flashes—check engine or low oil—we fix the situation. This is your dashboard saying, 'Warning, warning, system failure.' Is this starting to make sense how interconnected we are to the physical body and our three main emotional centres?

Including essential oils can help support you along your healing journey. They are nature's gifts to be cherished and respected for their healing abilities on an emotional, spiritual and physical level. The fragrance of essential oils can assist in calming and relaxing the mind while opening a guarded heart to the possibilities of love. Essential oils can comfort, nurture, hold your hand and assist in opening the door to your emotional healing journey. Reflecting back on my own experiences, essential oils gave me a feeling of being cradled and nurtured while I was facing my inner demons. It gave me a sense of belonging; a feeling that I was not alone. However, the individual must do their part in the healing process by looking inward, changing thinking patterns and moving forward by letting go of the past. This is a journey worth taking. How comforting it is to know nature is nurturing us along the way with these gifts from the earth.

To the outside world, my childhood appeared to be one filled with neglect. I was rarely bathed or wore clean clothes until the age of eleven. That's when I realised and took ownership over my hygiene and clothes. Our family nickname at school was Nash-trash, as Nash is my maiden name. Under all this was a dark secret that lay behind closed doors. I was sexually abused starting from the age of five until I was about nine when I started fighting back and trying to avoid vulnerable situations. I felt very unsafe in the world, always on alert of the next attack, from someone, anyone. I think I just accepted by this point that males treated females in this manner. It was our lot in life, our worth in the world—sex toys for males. Why did men feel like they had the right to violate me? My hatred toward men grew deep in my heart. My walls went flying up, shutting myself in for protection. This trend of sexual abuse continued into my high school years and beyond. I felt hopeless. I attempted suicide during that time but thanks to my cousin, I am still here today.

This set the groundwork for the false life scripts that would play out in my life. My experiences influenced my ability to trust others and my concepts of love and self-worth. I developed a fear of men and rejected my own emerging sexuality. I was hesitant to accept anything, fearing what payment would be required. I hid in shame, guilt and self-loathing. I oppressed my true self—that little girl with the blonde piggy tails and vibrant smile. I reflect back on a photo of myself at age six. There is no light in my eyes, no smile and a kind of vacant expression on my face. I had left the building.

Emotionally, I was unable to process and accept what was happening to me so I shut down. I accepted being a victim because I thought that was all I was worth. These false scripts were being confirmed continually by family, peers and society. This set me up for a life of abuse. It seemed most men in my life only wanted me for their own sexual gratification. This left me feeling like a piece of meat and that I was worth no better treatment. They must be right, I thought and continued to push my true self down. It is no surprise then that the relationships in my life confirmed these false belief systems. Even though they made me feel bad, I thought it was all I deserved; all I was worth.

I chose relationships and work environments that reaffirmed how I felt about myself; about how I deserved to be treated. The way you feel about yourself is the type of treatment you will accept from others. You will place yourself around people or in situations that fit these false self-beliefs you have about yourself. My journey is not unique. Our experiences—fears, self-worth, hate and love—are all universal as the human condition. This is your personal journey and only you can take control of your life. By picking up this book you have planted the seed of change and a new beginning. I encourage you to move past fear and live the life you deserve—full of love and abundance.

CHAPTER 2

How Do Essential Oils Assist In Emotional Healing?

It's well-documented through research that essential oils have a powerful healing effect on the physical body and the mind, but what about emotional healing? Our bodies are complex organisms that not only benefit physically from natural essential oils but all aspects of our wellbeing, including our emotions. When odour molecules of essential oils are inhaled, nerve impulses are stimulated by the olfactory bulb, sending a signal along the olfactory tract to the amygdala and hippocampus. The olfactory system is part of the limbic system, which serves many differing functions including processing long-term memories, emotions, desires, attention, hormones, regulating blood pressure and heart rate, as well as operating the autonomic nervous system. This in turn releases neuropeptides, hormones and neurotransmitters into the body. These impulses travel to five different areas of the brain, including the amygdala. This area of the brain stores and releases emotional trauma and is interconnected with the hippocampus, the long-term memory centre of the brain. Our body is made up of millions of cells; the chemical compound and size of some essential oil molecules can pass through the cell wall, directly interacting with brain cells. This means that some essential oils, like frankincense, are able to pass the blood brain barrier. Due to this close relationship, essential oils have profound physiological and psychological effects. This connection is the key to how essential oils tap into our emotions, memories and our subconscious. It is up to the individual to step through this open door to emotional healing and freedom with the helping hand of essential oils.

The same type of essential oil can have different chemical effects depending on the person, as our experiences and interpretations of life are so uniquely personal and subjective. For example, a particular person inhales the essential oil of peppermint, triggering the memory of her uncle's breath when he would come into her room at night unwelcome. This could bring feelings that may have been buried all these years to the surface. This individual inhaling the essential oil of peppermint could become agitated or angry but not be able to explain why they are feeling this way. They have totally blocked and suppressed their experiences of abuse with the uncle whose breath smelled like peppermint. This individual is aware on a subconscious level but has completely blocked it from conscious memory out of self-preservation. The body, mind and spirit are still holding on to all of the emotional trauma from the abuse; given enough time, these emotions will eventually manifest into disease. It takes energy for the body to suppress or hold down these emotional feelings. In the short-term, our brains are practicing self-preservation but in reality it is only creating a false sense of security. In the long-term, these suppressed emotions are a ticking time bomb that could explode at any time in various forms.

Alternatively, inhaling an essential oil such as rose can reduce fear, anxiety and the stress associated with emotional healing and everyday life. It may be that the essential oil fragrance brings back subconscious feelings of belonging and wellbeing as it interacts with the cells of the brain, producing a chemical reaction. It could have been the subtle scent of lavender that triggers a memory of your pretend tea party in the garden with your mother. These same feelings of safety are triggered when the essential oil fragrance is inhaled and processed through the memory centre of the brain. Hence, certain essential oils can put the body in a relaxed, calm frame of mind to work through the past emotional issues in life. This gives the person an opportunity to process and deal with their memories and emotions by taking a look at what untrue life scripts about their self-worth are running behind the scenes because of their life experiences. On the other hand, this person may feel like the pain is too much to bear and repress their feelings through addictions or destructive relationships with themselves and others, just to name a few. When we repress our feelings and emotions, eventually there is a price to pay and our body serves up the bill in the form of mental and physical diseases.

I am not suggesting that essential oils will emotionally heal on their own; they are only part of the puzzle. We have to take ownership of our emotions and look within for healing. Essential oils can assist in this process on an emotional level by giving us strength and courage. Metaphorically speaking, they hold your hand, cradle you and set the scene for emotional healing. Selecting essential oils can be a very personal experience and can change from day to day depending on what your body needs at the time. Certain essential oils are recommended for specific types of healing work as noted throughout this book. Your healing journey can be done without using essential oils. I personally choose to use these wonderful gifts from nature because they opened my heart, provided support and comforted me along the way. They allowed me to trust myself, release anger and accept my true self to live in freedom and joy.

What Are Essential Oils?

Essential oils are derived from the flower, rind, leaf, root, seed, resin, bark, etc. found in nature. The plant material is harvested and processed at a distillation facility where the essential oils are extracted. The most common method of extracting essential oils from plant material is steam distillation. In this method, steam is released into an extraction chamber where the plant material is held at the bottom. As the steam passes through the plant material, the essential oils rise with the steam into a cooling chamber. In the cooling chamber, the essential oils rise to the top as the water remains at the bottom. The cooling process allows the essential oils and the water to be separated naturally due to their chemical properties. The naturally occurring essential oils protect the plant from disease and predators. This built-in defence mechanism is part of the arsenal of chemicals utilised by the plant for protection. This defence system or life-force is present in the living essential oils compound that are pure, therapeutic grade quality. They have the same effect when used for our health and emotional wellbeing. For example, melaleuca essential oil guards against parasitic relationships and clears toxic, negative energies by creating an energetic field of protection. The use of essential oils has been well-documented throughout history; they have been used to defend against disease, remedy physical ailments, for emotional support, beauty treatments and spiritual ceremonies.

Does Essential Oil Quality Matter?

Not all essential oils are the same quality so caution should be used when trying to purchase 100% pure therapeutic grade essential oils. Many essential oils are diluted with alcohol, only have a small percentage of pure essential oil or are synthetically created substances from a laboratory. The geographic location, growing cycle and distillation process can alter the chemical composition of the essential oils, sometimes rendering them ineffective in a therapeutic context. Currently there are no government regulations on labelling essential oils to indicate their quality and chemical composition. For example, a bottle can be labelled as 'peppermint essential oil' but be missing the biological name *Mentha piperita*. Don't be misled, these are not pure essential oils and have no therapeutic benefit. Other labelling includes 'fragrant essential oil' or 'essential oil perfume'. These can be harmful and dangerous if applied to the body, inhaled or ingested.

Price can also be a clue to the quality of essential oils, but not always. If you purchase a two dollar bottle of rose, you can be sure it's synthetic. The amount of plant material needed for just 1 oz of pure rose essential oil is 60,000 flowers. Suppliers can also adulterate essential oils and still charge the same price as if they were 100% pure. Where money is involved and limited plant material available, unethical practices unfortunately occur. Do your research and purchase essential oils from a reputable supplier. Ask the supplier question like: What is the country of origin? How are the oils tested for purity? Are they independently tested and by whom? If a supplier says they are all natural and great quality but have no information to back their claims, adulteration is highly possible. A reputable, ethical company will be transparent and glad to provide any documentation supporting the quality of their essential oils.

Application Methods for Essential Oils

How can we effectively use essential oils to assist with emotional healing? The two ways I suggest are topical and aromatic. Topical application refers to the application of essential oils applied directly on the body. They can be applied neat, meaning no dilution, or in combination with a carrier oil like coconut or almond. I recommend applying 1–3 drops of essential oil on wrist, stomach, chest, back of the neck, behind the ears or bottom of the feet.

Aromatic usage refers to the inhalation of essential oils. This is the quickest and most powerful method and can affect hormones, memories and emotions within seconds. I recommend inhaling directly from the essential oil bottle or adding 3 drops of essential oil to a high frequency oscillation diffuser. This type of cool air diffuser releases a micro mist of essential oil and water into the air without heating. When heating therapeutic grade essential oils, it changes its chemical composition and limits its natural healing power.

Essential oils can be used singularly or in a synergic blend, which means two or more essential oils combined together. When two or more essential oils are combined, the synergising effect produces an essential oil blend greater than the individual essential oil properties. In essence, the properties of the essential oils are enhanced and changed by blending them together. When using essential oils singularly or blending them together, set a clear, positive intent of forgiveness or self-acceptance, depending on the required support needed at the time of application.

Like any product, essential oils need to be used appropriately, following safety guidelines and precautions specific to each oil. Consult your physician if taking any prescription medication as certain essential oils may interfere with these medications. When using citrus oils (e.g. bergamot, lemon, lime, orange and tangerine) or ginger, it is recommended that you avoid direct sunlight for a period of time after application. Care should also be taken to prevent direct contact with the eyes, nose and ears, as essential oils should never be put directly in or on these areas of the body. Other oils, such as cassia, cinnamon, thyme and oregano need to be diluted before applying directly to the body as they can create sensitivity. A list of safety precautions for adults, children and pregnant women can be found in the Essential Oil Safety Reference Chart in the back of this book.

CHAPTER 3

Who Am I? A Journey of Self-Discovery

Have you ever asked yourself the question, Who am I? Most of us have been perplexed with this question trying to find the answer. We find this question challenging to answer because we have abandoned our true selves on a conscious and subconscious level. The question 'Who am I?' is a good starting point to reconnect and explore who we truly are as a person. Write down the question, Who am I? Sit quietly with your thoughts. What emotions do you feel? What words come to mind? Write them down as these are all clues that will lead you to self-discovery; your true self. This may also help shed some light on the false beliefs and life scripts that may be running in your life. I will cover this topic in more depth in Chapter 5. The intensity of the emotions that come up during this exercise will signal you to explore those areas deeper. Keep on digging and push through the challenges. It's worth it; you are worth it. Keep breaking it down. If you are having trouble identifying an emotion, refer to the emotion chart in Chapter 4.

As you will see, I have included in the 'List of Your True Self' some traits we may view as negative. We all have them and living in delusion won't make them disappear. Too often we have hidden behind the mask of false illusion for so long that we even fool ourselves. View these insights as opportunities to change your behaviour patterns and embrace self-acceptance. Identifying how you feel about yourself can be confronting but becoming aware is the first step towards emotional healing. It puts the spotlight on the things you are trying desperately to hide. Loving and accepting yourself is the key to happiness. No one or nothing will ever fill that empty hole in your soul, though many people have tried to find solace at the bottom of a bottle, in a pack of Tim Tams or the never-ending work day. You are the only person that has the power over your own happiness. Not only is it unfair to put that onto another person but it is also destined to fail. It's about looking inward, loving ourselves and accepting who you are as a person; that is how to find true happiness. Until you love your true self—the good, the bad and the ugly—you will always be drifting in the night. You will continue searching, even though the answer is right in front of you—love and self-acceptance.

If you're finding this exercise difficult, start with writing factual information about yourself that cannot be disputed. My name is Jane Susan Doe, I am fifty-six years old and I was born in South Port, North Carolina. I volunteer at the pet shelter and work as a beautician. I enjoy painting portraits of family members and working in the garden. From looking at the above information about Jane, she could be described as patient, caring, empathetic, compassionate, nurturing, responsible, creative, dependable, artistic, expressive, etc.

Another strategy is to ask a trusted family member or friend to write down a few words that describe who you are in their eyes. This not only gives you some insight into your true self but also encouragement from a loved one.

Make a List of Your True Self

- Loving
- Patient
- Funny
- Intelligent
- Innovative
- Caring
- Spiritual
- Sensual
- Empathetic
- Practical
- Realistic
- Flexible
- Loyal
- Thrifty
- Honest
- Resilient
- Artistic
- Responsible
- Creative
- Sensitive
- Other-centred
- Transparent
- Genuine
- Respectful
- Intuitive
- Devoted
- Courageous
- Brave
- Expressive
- Sympathetic
- Organised
- Nurturing
- Affectionate
- Inquisitive
- Erotic
- Inventive
- Spontaneous
- Empowered
- Dependable
- Outgoing
- Playful
- Controlling
- Selfish
- Manipulative
- Judgemental
- Materialistic

Affirmations

- My feelings matter
- I will not put up with being treated poorly
- I deserve to be heard and acknowledged
- I will not walk on eggshells or blame myself
- I have the right to be treated with respect, valued and wanted in good times and bad
- I deserve consideration for my feelings and journey
- I will not beg for attention. I am worth more than that. I deserve more than that
- I will not take a back seat in my life. I will heal and move forward
- I embrace the person I am and all the wonderful things I have to offer

- I will not hide or be ashamed of who I am or what I have been through
- This is my journey and I choose growth, life and forgiveness
- I choose me because I am worth it; every part of me and everything I have to offer
- I will not hide from my problems. I will embrace them, deal with them and move forward

Intuition

What is intuition? It has been described as a gut feeling, a sense of knowing or a feeling that something is just not right. I describe intuition as our body, mind and spirit's ability to access universal knowledge anytime, anywhere. We can all tap into this universal knowledge; this powerful energy that surrounds us and is in everything. This energy has been called the Holy Spirit, Mother Earth, The Creator and God. How you refer to this energy is a personal choice. We have become so disconnected with this energy and our intuition that we often make choices out of fear, anger or pride.

There was a time in my life that I proclaimed my intuition was non-existent. I think back and have a little chuckle at how far I've come on my journey of healing and enlightenment. This was a life script that I changed from 'I do not have an intuition' to 'I embrace and acknowledge my intuition as a beautiful gift from the universe to be treasured and respected'. It took me awhile to trust myself and the knowledge that was freely given. At first I would argue with or second-guess myself because I wanted to do something different, my way. I wanted to hold on to that false sense of control that had been so destructive in my life.

We don't always want to listen to our intuition, especially when it goes against something we want or don't want. You may meet a potential partner but have that gut feeling not to get involved. You want to believe that person is good and what they are telling you is the truth, but your intuition is saying, 'Run like hell!' We want to believe in the fantasy, the fairy-tale. Maybe you are lonely and think this person will make you happy. So you turn a blind eye to their real behaviour because you want to believe the lies and the false illusion of possible future happiness. You have two choices: take the hard road, full of road blocks and heart ache; or listen to your intuition and be guided in the best direction.

Once I was hiking and my intuition said, 'Go left.' Now I could have went either way, as the trails intertwined all over the area. I argued and thought, No, I am going my way! About 10 feet down the path, I got the message again, 'Go the other way.' Again, I wanted control so I kept walking. I walked another 10 feet down the path, but this time the message was stronger, more urgent, 'Go the other way!' Fine, fine, okay! I turned around, walked back the 20 feet and went left on the track.

I never found out why I was supposed to go left on the hiking track that day. Maybe there was a poisonous snake or an unsavoury person, it really does not matter because I trusted my intuition. Every time I listen, abundance follows and life flows easily through me. I could not imagine life without this guidance. Actually, I can, because that was my reality for many, many years. By blocking the sexual abuse and other emotional traumas in my life, I also blocked my intuition. By opening your heart to emotional healing, you are opening the door to your intuition.

How do you know it's your intuition and not your ego trying to bully its way back into control? What feeling or message are you getting from your intuition? Be a detective in your life. Ask yourself, What effect will my actions have on myself or others? What is my motivation? Will it be harmful to myself or others? Maybe they are emotional responses to past experiences ... unprocessed emotions from the past can resurface in new situations without warrant. I experienced this when a friend asked if I was interested in being fixed up with one of her male friends. I agreed to the arrangement because I had opened my heart to love and was feeling ready to trust myself again. I felt my intuition saying it was time to take the next step to embrace love. Later that day, I started to think about the situation and my anxiety kicked in full force. What's going on? My mind started to bully me about past relationship mistakes, the poor choices I had made with previous partners and the behaviours I tolerated. I started to question my intuition. Was I ready? Is my intuition now telling me to run?

I regained control of my thoughts, replacing the negative, destructive ones with positive encouragement. I repeated affirmations: I am only surrounded by love. My thoughts are calm and comforting. I only have thoughts that support me. I forgive myself and others. I let go of the past and embrace the present. Yes, I was back in control of my thoughts!

Now, with a clear mind, I started to be a detective, questioning myself: Is this anxiety real? Where is it coming from? What has caused this reaction? To answer the question, my anxiety was not from the current situation. It was a reaction to previous events that had happened in the past that caused the emotional response of anxiety to rear its ugly head. My mind jumped right on board with the previous knowledge from similar situations to conclude the outcome of my future interactions. My mind was being 'helpful' by replaying these past similar situations, which induced the current unfounded anxiety I was feeling. I had never met or spoken to this person before, it was the sheer fact that he was a man who could potentially be an intimate partner. My anxiety had no basis in this current situation. I could trust my intuition and know these feelings were really coming from a fear of the past.

I dug a little deeper to find out what else might be going on. What was I still hiding from? I started to free write in my journal whatever came to my mind. I had previously replaced old, false life scripts: 'All men are evil. It's unsafe to be alone with men. I am shameful. Men only want sex'. However, I had never looked at how I actually felt about the act of sex. My false beliefs about sex had not been challenged. I changed 'Sex is dirty, shameful, degrading, abusive, violating and demeaning' to 'Sex is beautiful, empowering, expressive, intimate, passionate and loving'. What a change to how I felt, the anxiety had lifted—gone.

Recommended Essential Oils

- Bergamot
- Black pepper
- Clary sage
- Jasmine
- Lemon
- Melissa
- Rosemary
- Spearmint
- Ylang ylang
- Wintergreen

These essential oils can be used singularly or in combinations. For topical application, place 1–3 drops on wrists, back of the neck or bottom of the feet. Inhale directly from the bottle or add 3 drops to a diffuser.

CHAPTER 4

Emotions

Emotions are chemical reactions produced in the body from hormones and stored memory responses in the conscious and sub-conscious mind. Emotions are something we all experience as human beings. You could be having an argument with another person and start to feel threatened. Your sympathetic nervous system kicks into flight or fight mode, releasing adrenaline and other hormones. Your body registers this new information and taps into stored emotions from similar situations. This process happens within a split second without effort from your conscious mind. Sometimes we don't even know how to express our emotions in words, as it may be a foreign concept in our family, circle of friends or community groups. We feel numb and disconnected, feverishly attempting to push down and block our emotions, thinking they will just go away. We are taught at an early age how to suppress our emotions, pretend everything is fine and hide behind a false mask of denial. If we open our hearts to healing and self-acceptance, the false mask will release and fall away, giving us a sense of wholeness.

How many times has someone asked you how you were feeling and you stated, 'Fine,' when really, deep down, you were tormented by guilt or shame? We put on the 'everything is okay' mask, burying our feelings and emotions even deeper from our true selves. Sometimes we focus on other people's problems and issues under the pretence of helping them but we are really only trying to distract ourselves from looking within. This is temporary, of course, as we can only push down our emotions for so long before they manifest into illness and disease. So why do we behave in a way that is detrimental to our health and emotional wellbeing? *Fear.*

What *is* fear? Why does it have such a powerful and profound effect on our lives? It's just a word really—fear. I challenge you today to take back the power from your fear. It's only as powerful in our lives as we let it become. When thoughts of fear creep into your mind, replace them with thoughts of love. If you proclaim love enough times over fear, love will become your automatic thought as it becomes a new, positive habit in your life.

Our mind and body have another mechanism in play that was useful in early civilisation—detachment. You can also see this play out in the animal kingdom. When a human or animal is being eaten alive, they detach themselves from the experience. They check out and put up the 'Out to Lunch' sign. This phenomenon also happens when we are put in emotional situations that we can't handle at the moment. We mentally can't handle the situation, don't process it and push it deep down. This is our subconscious' way of protecting us in the present moment but is unbeneficial for us in the long-term. Most of the time we don't even know it's buried until we get physical or emotional symptoms as it tries to resurface in the conscious mind. Look at this as an opportunity to heal—a blessing.

What are our emotions telling us? It can be hard to identify how we are truly feeling, especially if we don't have the vocabulary to describe it. With only a few words to describe our feelings—such as fear, sad, anger, joy—we can block the healing process. Dig deeper, ask yourself questions: Why am I angry? What do I fear? Be a detective in your own life. It will be challenging to ask yourself these questions on a deeper level but that is where the deep healing can begin. If you start feeling scared or fearful when exploring a certain topic, that is when it is most beneficial to push deeper in that area. Your body is sending signals that say, 'Hey, don't look in there, keep that door closed.' Essential oils can help calm and support you on an emotional level during this process. It's as simple as inhaling essential oil directly from the bottle or applying a few drops to your wrist. Fear and anxiety come in from the unknown. Your mind starts to doubt itself and tells you, 'This is just too much.' It tries to distract you with other fears and thoughts. If you abandon ship and allow your mind to get distracted by meaningless thoughts, all your pain and suffering remains. It has already manifested in physical or emotional pain in your life or you wouldn't be searching for emotional healing. I will let you in on a little secret: once you push through that fear of the unknown and that fear of what's hiding behind the mask of false illusion, healing happens—true emotional healing and self-acceptance at the core of your being. The pain and fear melt away, leaving you wondering why you waited so long.

The six core emotions are anger, fear, surprise, happy, sad and disgust. These can then be broken down further as listed below.

Anger

- Critical
- Sceptical
- Sarcastic
- Distant
- Suspicious
- Withdrawn
- Frustrated
- Irritated

- Infuriated
- Aggressive
- Hostile
- Provoked
- Mad
- Enraged
- Furious
- Hateful

- Violated
- Resentful
- Threatened
- Jealous
- Insecure
- Hurt
- Devastated
- Embarrassed

Fear

- Humiliated
- Ridiculed
- Disrespected
- Rejected
- Alienated
- Inadequate

- Submissive
- Insignificant
- Worthless
- Insecure
- Inferior
- Inadequate

- Anxious
- Worried
- Overwhelmed
- Scared
- Frightened
- Terrified

Surprise

- Startled
- Shocked
- Dismayed
- Confused

- Disillusioned
- Perplexed
- Amazed
- Astonished

- Awed
- Excited
- Eager
- Energetic

Happy

- Optimistic
- Inspired
- Open
- Intimate
- Playful
- Sensitive
- Peaceful
- Hopeful

- Loving
- Powerful
- Provocative
- Courageous
- Accepted
- Respected
- Fulfilled
- Proud

- Important
- Confident
- Interested
- Amused
- Inquisitive
- Joyful
- Liberated
- Ecstatic

Sad

- Bored
- Apathetic
- Indifferent
- Lonely
- Abandoned
- Isolated

- Depressed
- Inferior
- Empty
- Despaired
- Powerless
- Vulnerable

- Miserable
- Ignored
- Victimised
- Guilty
- Remorseful
- Ashamed

Disgust

- Avoidance
- Aversion
- Hesitant
- Awful
- Revulsion
- Detestable
- Disappointed
- Repugnant
- Revolted
- Disapproving
- Loathing
- Judgemental

Recommended Essential Oils

Anger

- Bergamot
- Cedarwood
- Geranium
- Lavender
- Thyme
- Ylang Ylang

Apply 1–3 drops topically on the chest or bottom of the feet.

Fear

- Birch
- Cassia
- Cinnamon
- Clary Sage
- Cypress
- Juniper Berry
- Lavender
- Myrrh
- Orange
- Sandalwood

Apply 1–3 drops topically on the upper and lower stomach.

Surprise

- Basil
- Clary Sage
- Lavender
- Lemon
- Peppermint
- Rosemary
- Wintergreen

Apply 1–3 drops topically on the chest or bottom of the feet.

Happy

- Bergamot
- Lemon
- Lime
- Melissa
- Orange
- Roman Chamomile
- Tangerine
- Ylang Ylang

Apply 1–3 drops topically on the upper stomach.

Sad

- Bergamot
- Clary Sage
- Eucalyptus
- Geranium
- Juniper Berry
- Lavender
- Lemon
- Peppermint
- Ylang Ylang

Apply 1–3 drops topically on the chest, lower and upper stomach or bottom of the feet.

Disgust

- Black Pepper
- Geranium
- Helichrysum
- Juniper Berry
- Lemon
- Peppermint
- Rose
- Vetiver
- Ylang Ylang

Apply 1–3 drops topically on the upper stomach.

All of the essential oils mentioned above can be inhaled directly from the bottle throughout the day as needed. Refer to the Essential Oils Safety Reference Chart in the back of this book for precautionary guidelines.

CHAPTER 5
Life Scripts

What are life scripts? They are a set of beliefs about who we are as a person that determines how we view ourselves and the world around us. They are an accumulation of self-interpretations and perceptions others have placed on us. These life scripts are unusually well-cemented by the time we are five years of age and can have positive and negative effects on our lives. Part of our human survival is to store away emotions and feelings we cannot handle as a form of self-preservation. It may have been effective when we had to worry about being attacked by predatory animals but we now live in a different time. Our mind buries these emotions and unless we dig them up and deal with them, they slowly eat away manifesting into a disease or illness. These life scripts have been running for a long time, depending on your age. They are so deeply ingrained in our subconscious that we don't even realise they automatically and continually play out in our lives. Exposing these negative life scripts and replacing them with the truth is the path to emotional healing and wellbeing.

What patterns have we taken on from our parents, grandparents, teachers, etc.? Their beliefs about the world, themselves, relationships and you? They all influence what we inherently think about the world we live in and ourselves on a conscious and subconscious level. We tend to repeat the same cycles and usually don't ever stop to question why. It's just what we have always done, who we are. Even if you're unhappy with the life scripts running in your life, they are continually repeated unless you challenge them.

Start to question these self-beliefs and ask yourself, Are they true? Do they bring me joy, love and acceptance or do they bring me misery, sorrow and fear? You can break these negative cycles and retrain your mind. The question is: Do you feel you deserve to be happy? We as human beings seek approval from others and a connection to our community. We put on a false mask to fit what is expected from our interactions with others and the world. Sometimes this false mask gives us a sense of approval and connection, but in reality it's creating a further disconnect from our true self and the world. This causes the opposite effect, hindering our happiness as we dishonour our true self. Letting go of past beliefs allows us to live in the present and lets the future unfold.

Are you holding onto life scripts that are untrue? Have you been judged negatively by someone, possibly out of anger, and it stuck as a core belief? Have you been holding onto information about yourself that others have projected onto you unintentionally or because of their unresolved issues? 'Don't be so stupid, just go sit down and shut up!' This can instil negative life scripts: I am stupid and dumb. I am worthless. I don't have anything valuable to say. I am weak, insecure and rejected. By no means am I saying that you should blame your parents for your problems. We are responsible for our own choices and consequences. We are all human beings and we all make mistakes in life. Instead, express empathy and compassion to others on their journey and judge no one unless you have walked a mile in their shoes. We tend to take on the beliefs of others without much consideration; including generational life scripts, like your mother repeating, 'We are so poor and will never have any money.' Even if these scripts make us feel bad, we tend to seek out relationships and situations that reinforce these false self-beliefs about who we are as a person.

Start by exploring the way you were born, how you were as a toddler and your early school years. If possible, ask your mother or father what you were like as a child. Often those early years in life can be a blank in our current consciousness. In saying that, our subconscious mind remembers everything—emotions, smells, sounds—and stores them away for later reference. Sometimes we are unable to process this information so it is pushed down for the time being. Our mind buries the unprocessed information, thinking this would protect us from harm but it will always resurface in some form of physical or emotional issue as we get older. We disconnect from our true self, emotions and feelings. Over time we can forget who we truly are as a person and accept the false life scripts that have been projected on our lives.

Take an objective look at your thought patterns. What are they? What are your core beliefs about the world? What patterns or life scripts can you identify? What type of people and situations keep coming back into your life with the same results? Ask yourself questions and observe your internal self-talk and the statements you make about your life. These are all clues about what you believe about yourself on a conscious and unconscious level.

In my own life, I proudly proclaim, 'The only person I can rely on is myself.' There is an inherent flaw in this statement that goes against the core of who we are as human beings. We desire connection, contact and community for our physical and emotional wellbeing. I created situations and relationships in my life that fit this false life script I held about myself. I felt disconnected, alone, overwhelmed, unloved and hopeless, desperately trying to control everything and keep it together. When I could not obtain this unrealistic goal, I fell into depression, self-punishment and unhealthy relationships. It was not until I rewrote these negative, false life scripts and replaced them with positive, true life scripts that my emotional healing began.

The false, negative life scripts will try to creep back into your mind. They have become habitual ways of thinking and processing your world. Be patient and kind to yourself. When these destructive thought patterns enter your mind, keep replacing them with the new, positive life scripts and eventually they will become the habit of your thought patterns. Refer to the chart below for some common false life scripts and suggestions for replacing them with positive life scripts. These are just examples and I always encourage you to follow your own intuition and path when finding the affirmations that connect with your soul.

Set clear intentions and be specific about the life scripts you want to change. Use the list provided to give you some ideas of how to replace negative life scripts with positive, productive ones. While you are replacing the old life scripts, cultivate an emotional response that supports these new life scripts. If it comes from hate, cultivate the emotional feeling of being loved. If it comes from fear, cultivate the emotional feelings of being safe.

You must be vigilant with replacing the well-worn neurological connections. It will take time and repetition to tip the scales from old life scripts to new ones. Think of it as an old goat track. Over the years it has been worn down to dirt, ingrained into the ground, easy to follow without even thinking about it. When the goats decide to follow a new path, they have to wear down the grass and remember where the new path goes. They may even go back to the old path out of habit and security. Over time, the old path becomes overgrown and the new path is easy to follow; it has become the new habit. It is the same with your thought patterns; over time, you will create new paths and habits in your thinking and let go of the old, negative habits. It takes twenty-one days to replace an old habit with a new habit. It is very important to replace the old life scripts with new, positive reflections of your true self. If you just think, I don't want to feel fear anymore, go away, but don't replace it with anything, it will just gravitate back to fear, because that's what it knows.

The ego won't like giving up control. There is a sense of the unknown, fear and breaking out of your comfort zone. You will be challenged by past memories that validate the old life scripts that ran automatically in your life, trying to make you feel guilt or second-guess yourself. Acknowledge and accept that you cannot change the past or control the future but you do have control over your present thoughts. Forgive yourself and others; release the old so there is space to welcome the new. Replacing your life scripts in the morning creates your intentions for the day and empowers your awareness to the possibilities of life. Replacing your life scripts in the evening right before you fall asleep assists in bridging the gap between the conscious and subconscious mind. This is an important step as the majority of our thoughts and actions come from the unconscious mind. Identifying our thought patterns is a step towards understanding ourselves. This understanding can be the gateway to emotional healing and allowing yourself to have a life filled with joy, love and positivity. The negative, destructive thoughts are listed in the left column and the positive, productive replacements are listed in the right column.

False, Negative Life Scripts	Rewrite to True, Positive Life Scripts
I am dumb and stupid	I am smart and intelligent
I am unlovable	I am loveable
I am not good enough	I am good enough
The world is full of evil	The world is full of good
I am ugly	I am beautiful and magnificent
I am a victim	I am a survivor

False, Negative Life Scripts	Rewrite to True, Positive Life Scripts
I am worthless	I am worthy
Success means making a lot of money	I define success on my own terms
I don't belong anywhere	I belong to the community of the world
I am shameful	I am full of acceptance and self-love
I don't deserve to be alive	I am free to live my life in abundance
I am not respectable	I am respected
I can only rely on myself	I can rely on myself and others
I am dirty	I am clean and natural
Life is too hard	Life flows easily
Change is too hard	Change is easy and rewarding
I hate myself	I love myself
I am never heard	I have a voice and speak up for what I believe in
I reject myself	I accept myself
The world is unsafe	The world is safe, I am safe in the world
I am inadequate	I am adequate in all areas of my life
I trust no one, not even myself	I trust myself, I trust my intuition, I trust others
I am angry	I am peaceful and calm
I deserve to be punished	I nurture myself
I am weak	I am strong and resilient
I cannot change	I easily accept change
I am alone	I am surrounded by love and positive energy

False, Negative Life Scripts	Rewrite to True, Positive Life Scripts
I am hopeless	I am hopeful
I am powerless	I am powerful, I keep my personal power
I am fearful of men/women	I am safe around men/women
Money is the root of all evil	Money is just an object
Bad things always happen to me	Good things always happen to me
I always struggle with money	My life is full of abundance in all areas
I am insecure	I am secure in my true self, I love me
All men/women are evil	All human beings have the potential for good

Recommended Essential Oils

- Bergamot
- Black Pepper
- Cilantro
- Clary Sage
- Coriander
- Frankincense
- Ginger
- Lemongrass
- Thyme
- Vetiver
- White Fir

These essential oils can be used singularly or in combinations. Apply 1–3 drops topically on the chest, upper stomach or bottom of the feet. Inhale directly from the bottle throughout the day as needed or add 1–3 drops to a diffuser.

CHAPTER 6

Self-Sabotage

Self-sabotage is mostly a subconscious process where we think and act in ways that prevent personal growth. The opportunity may be applying for a new job, trusting in another person or following your passion. We may be capable and qualified to embrace these opportunities that life presents but because of self-doubt, fear, etc. we fail to act or we create road blocks that make it impossible to move forward. Why do we self-sabotage when we are on the brink of success or an emotional breakthrough? Where are these insecurities and fears coming from? It has to do with how we truly feel about ourselves and the life scripts that play out in our lives. If we have always been told we are worthless, we will take that on as our true self, even if it's not true. We will even say it about ourselves and create situations where we feel worthless. This also applies to the types of relationships we have with other people. We tend to bring people into our lives that confirm these negative self-beliefs because we feel that is all we deserve. Of course, this is not true and makes us feel bad, but it's all we know; it's comfortable. However, you can stop the self-sabotage by separating yourself from what other people in your life have dumped on you because of their own life scripts and beliefs.

We self-sabotage in many different ways. Have you ever caught yourself saying, 'I just don't have the time, I am too busy.' Give yourself a reality check; you can make time for yourself. Turn off the television, log off social media and step away from the phone. You can always make time, even if it's just five minutes here and there throughout the day. Even taking as little as a minute while you're washing your hands to say, 'I love you,' to the mirror. You matter. Respect yourself. Make your physical and emotional health a priority in life.

This book has been a learning experience for me, including this chapter on self-sabotage. I have doubted myself and my abilities all my life but I know on an intuitive, spiritual level that this is my path. I wanted to write but was finding I was busying myself with non-productive work and procrastinating. So I asked myself, Why? What is holding me back from writing? The answer came back loud and clear: Doubt. I was doubting my abilities, knowledge and skills. Again, I asked myself, Why? It was because I thought I was not smart enough, not able to speak up for myself and didn't have anything worth saying. It was those old life scripts again, trying to creep in and sabotage my life. Luckily, using the skills and strategies in this book, I was able to be aware of what was happening and question my actions and motives. You too can gain these skills of self-awareness and be a detective in your own life to help reveal your own self-sabotaging tendencies.

Self-Distraction

It feels like we are hardwired to avoid taking a deep look at our emotional issues. This is why meditation is so valuable, as it helps us to have more awareness and control over our thoughts and actions. When looking at our true selves, the mind will try to distract and sabotage us from looking deep within ourselves. We start looking at other people and their issues, judging them and trying to solve their problems. Up on our high horse, looking at everyone else to take the focus off ourselves and distract us from dealing with buried emotions or traumas. This is the normal response if we live unaware of our behaviours; the mind is very tricky and can be a bit of a bully. The mind will try to prevent us, at all costs, from being hurt in the short-term. This concept is inherently flawed. It only pushes down these emotions, but they will resurface over and over again until we acknowledge, heal and move forward.

Our decisions and choices determine our actions and the type of person we become in life. The past and present circumstances don't have to define your future self. By creating new thoughts and actions, you can create a new life and live out your full potential. You have a choice to live in denial and self-deception about your life situation or look behind your mask of false illusion and embrace your true self. I lived in denial and was not even aware of it at the time. When we look inward to discover our true self, everything becomes clearer. Regular meditation helps to keep the mind focused, clear and able to discover the underlining motives for what you are feeling or the way you are behaving in a situation.

There will be triggers in life that will test your belief systems and challenge your progress. They try to sneak in the back door, so to speak. This is a great opportunity to ask: Why have I created this in my life? What lesson is this situation trying to tell me? What can I do to become more balanced? Have I stopped meditation, affirmations, body relaxing, journaling, etc.? Have compassion for yourself and others during these times of trial. Focus on the positives and what you can learn to move forward in your journey. If we take a view that life is about the journey not the destination, we can relax and start enjoying life here and now. This is where life is really happening all around us, all the time, the present moment. Feeling helpless about your situation in life and unwilling to change your behaviours will keep you stuck. Without changing your behaviours, you will have the same outcomes. We can blame others, complain or put up obstacles that we know will cause us to fail. This goes back to the false beliefs we have about ourselves and the world around us. If we feel this is all we are worth or if we feel hard done by life, this will manifest in our life. Until we are aware of our thought patterns, they run unchecked and follow these scripts at our own detriment. The great news is we have the power to change—change the way we think, act and feel about ourselves.

Recommended Essential Oils

- Black Pepper
- Cassia
- Fennel
- Frankincense
- Ginger
- Lemon
- Marjoram
- Melaleuca
- Peppermint
- Rosemary
- White Fir

These essential oils can be used singularly or in combinations. Apply 1–3 drops topically on the stomach, wrists or bottom of the feet. Inhale directly from the bottle throughout the day as needed or add 1–3 drops to a diffuser.

CHAPTER 7
Body Image

When you look in the mirror, how do you feel about your body and the way you look? As you stand in front of the mirror, what are the internal messages you repeat to yourself day after day? Do they build you up and encourage your inner goddess, leaving you feeling beautiful or do you rip yourself to shreds, belittling yourself until you feel degraded and hopeless?

The more we have a particular thought or thought pattern, the stronger and more ingrained it will become, eventually creating a habit. Our thoughts directly influence our self-worth and how we perceive ourselves. What we think and feel about ourselves also de-termines how we let other people treat us in life. If we tell ourselves that we are useless, worthless, fat and ugly, then we will project that image to others. Their behaviour towards us will fit the negative life scripts that we have about ourselves so we will allow them to treat us badly instead of standing up to them. It feels comfortable—*miserable* but comfortable; that's all we have known. However, we can change the false beliefs we have ingrained over the years. It starts with one thought at a time, which turns into two and so on until we automati-cally replace the negative self-talk with positive affirmations. This will create a positive difference in how we feel about ourselves and how we allow others to treat us.

In our society, there is an unrealistic perception of what beauty is in relation to body image. These scripts were developed early in life from family, peers, media and society. As a female, it appears our worth can only be measured in terms of external beauty. Magazines and television are filled with unrealistic portrayals of physically beautiful women. This can even be instilled by people who love and care about us, accidentally or in a non-malicious way. Our mothers can have a major impact on how we view beauty. Little ears hear and take on everything their parents say and do. A little girl might watch her mother in front of the mirror picking herself apart, stating how fat her legs are when in reality they are average size. The little girl's perception has now been imprinted to think average size legs are fat. You see a little girl in a cute dress and it's almost automatic: 'Oh, look how pretty she is! What a beautiful little girl.' There is nothing wrong with that but how often do we go deeper and compliment their intellectual abilities or physical accomplishments? This instils early on for that little girl the importance of outward beauty. This perception is then backed up by the media and other cultural influences. It is what forms the basis of who we are and how we view the world and ourselves.

I can remember that as a teenager I had a whole wall dedicated to pictures cut out of magazines. Of course, in all of the pictures the women were super skinny, had long hair and a perfect complexion, but that's not reality. I was striving for something that was unattainable and unrealistic. This is how I was judging myself, by using these artificially-created standards of beauty. Women and men come in all shapes and sizes; that is what makes human beings so special. There is beauty in all of us. The focus needs to shift to promote healthy bodies, inner beauty and self-acceptance instead of continuing to value physical appearance only. When you are taking care of your body, eating the right foods, exercising, resting and drinking enough water, the body will regulate to a healthy state and size that is right for you. We need to focus on what makes us each special and unique, not what we perceive to be our flaws.

Don't focus on the number on the bathroom scales but how your body feels. Do you have energy and vitality? It's about self-acceptance and being healthy. Can you be happy at any weight? Of course, happiness comes from within and from self-acceptance. Can you be healthy at any weight? Statistically speaking, when we carry excess weight, it causes a host of medical issues such as high blood pressure, heart disease and diabetes, just to name a few. If you excessively overeat, ask yourself, Why? Focus on what emotional needs you are trying to fill by overeating. Is it guilt, self-acceptance, shame, self-sabotage, unrealistic expectations or self-protection? Look at the patterns in your life. Do you eat when something is stressing you out? Do you eat unhealthy food as a reward? Do you binge eat to fill the need to feel loved? Keep asking yourself questions and journal about how you are feeling before, during and after you overeat. Do you feel guilt? Do you judge yourself? Do you think you have no self-control? Do you loathe the way you look in the mirror? Emotional eating has been referred to as 'trying to fill an emotional hole with food'. Overeating can be associated with low self-worth and self-punishment—in essence, slowly trying to kill yourself with food. Has your inner voice convinced you that this is respecting your body and living as your true self? When you look in the mirror, what does your inner voice tell you? 'I am so fat and ugly. Look at my stomach, it's so big, gross and ugly.' Stop punishing yourself! If the body is burdened with processed junk food, sugary soft drink and excessive amounts of food, combined with a sedentary lifestyle, it will have a negative effect on your health. We can also get addicted to the high from sugary carbohydrate-rich foods like cakes and cookies, contributing to the cycle of self-abuse.

A person can have a distorted body image at any weight. Someone with anorexia looks in the mirror and sees an overweight person, even though in reality they may be just skin and bones. A person in a normal weight range might also see an overweight person when they look in the mirror. Again, it comes back to how we feel about ourselves, even if in not reality. This obsession and control over our bodies is accomplished through excessive intake of food and not exercising; or, at the other end of the scale, very strict food intake and strenuous amounts of physical activity. It's our mental perceptions of reality and how we feel about ourselves—our true self—that determines what we think about our body. Ask yourself, Is this true? What is the reality of my physical being? Am I respecting myself? If not, ask yourself, Why? Keep digging for answers until you find the root of the emotions attached to these behaviours.

How will you know what it looks like if you have never experienced it before in your life? Ask yourself, Do I want to remain a victim and continue punishing myself or do I want to choose to be healthy and respect myself? Now is the time for change and that change comes from within. You will have a hard time feeling accepted if you don't accept yourself. Change your thinking patterns and let go of guilt, shame, self-punishment, self-hatred, control and disconnection from sexuality. The cycle can stop with you. What do you choose?

Recommended Essential Oils

- Bergamot
- Cilantro
- Ginger
- Grapefruit
- Lemon
- Patchouli
- Thyme

These essential oils can be used singularly or in combinations. Apply 1–3 drops topically on the stomach, wrists or bottom of the feet. Inhale directly from the bottle throughout the day as needed or add 1–3 drops to a diffuser.

Apply massage blend to the stomach, butt, hips and thighs:
- 20ml carrier oil (olive, almond or coconut)
- 2 drops grapefruit
- 2 drops ginger
- 2 drops lemon

CHAPTER 8
Negative and Positive Thought Patterns

Have you ever questioned your thoughts? Sit quietly for a few minutes and observe your thoughts. Are they mostly positive or negative thoughts? Where are your thoughts coming from? When contemplating, do you look at things from a negative perspective, a place of self-pity?

I played the 'poor as me' victim card many times in my life when I felt hopeless. I would focus on all the negative things happening in my life, complain about them and change nothing. I remained feeling hopeless, victimised and defeated. It was not until I starting looking at all the beautiful abundance in my life that my perceptions and thought patterns started to change. A negative mind will never give you a positive life. Make a conscious choice to have a positive attitude and cut negativity out of your life. By looking for the positive in every part of your life, it's natural to feel content and full of joy. That is the power of positive thinking.

I firmly believe that what we put out into the universe manifests in our own lives. If we are always thinking and speaking in negative ways, we will have a life filled with negativity. On the flip side, if we think positively and speak in positive terms, our life will be blessed with positivity. It's a simple formula that works and it is a universal law of nature. Imagine if your first thought when you wake up in the morning is, I hate this house. Why can't I live in a better place? I feel so fat from eating chocolate last night. I am so weak and disgusting. No wonder no one loves me. Take a guess how you are going to feel about yourself and your life. Think in the long-term, if you keep up this negative self-talk hour after hour, day after day, year after year, how do you think it will affect your self-esteem? Do you get the point? Instead, when you wake up in the morning and open your eyes, think how grateful you are to see the beautiful sunrise with the birds flying through the sky. Think about how you can physically get out of bed, you have a roof over your head and electricity to keep you warm; the list is endless. Even if there are things you can't do, focus on what you *can* do. You can tell yourself how beautiful you are inside and out. How blessed you are to have abundance in every area of your life. Now take a guess how you might be feeling about your life and your situation. You will feel more satisfied with yourself and your life. It all starts with changing that first negative thought and replacing it with a positive thought. One thought at a time and before you know it, your life will be full of abundance and you will love yourself.

In the same vein, gossip and talking negative about others is just as destructive. I know this may sound like Basics 101 but it is rampant in all levels of business, government, school and society. What is it that we gain from putting other people down? Some people do it to make themselves feel better but is that really the result of this conduct? They may feel superior or in control temporarily but it never lasts long or changes how that person truly feels about themselves. It just gives them a diversion so they don't have to look at themselves or their behaviour patterns. The next time you think about saying something negative about another person, replace it with a positive comment or simply don't say anything at all. Positivity is contagious. When you're interacting with a person who is tearing someone down, change the focus to something positive or remove yourself from the situation.

This concept also holds true for negative energies or pests in the form of negative people. Negativity breeds negativity and positivity breeds positivity; this is probably not the first time you have heard this saying. The kind of people you want in your life is your choice. I have cut toxic and negative people from my own life and have not looked back. For me, it has been an empowering experience to stand up for myself and know that I am worthy of more. Ask yourself, Who do I hang around with? Vampires, who suck everyone's energies and leave them feeling drained? Excessive givers, who take care of everyone else and never look after themselves? Rescuers, who try to save everyone else, even when they are drowning in their own delusion? Victims, who always say they are hard done by, even though they continuously allow themselves to be controlled? Takers, who demand everyone's time and energy and leave them feeling used? Negative people, who never see the positive side to anything?

Now ask yourself, What role do I play? Do I help others at the expensive of my own physical and mental health? Do I always run other people down in an attempt to make myself feel better? Do I always give and find it difficult to accept anything? These are just some examples to help provide some insight on excessive behaviours and how they can impact how we feel about ourselves and others. Relationships go through different stages and there are times when you will need to switch back and forth between roles. This is part of the natural flow of a balanced relationship. It becomes detrimental when it's always to one extreme or the other. By asking yourself these hard-hitting questions, it will help you in determining what types of relationships you allow in your life. It also put the ownership of your own behaviour to the forefront to peel back the layers of your own behaviour patterns and life scripts. Our behaviour and thought patterns will attract like-minded people into our worlds. We can change and it starts with our thoughts; they turn into words; they manifest into actions. What type of person do you choose to embrace?

Gratefulness

What is gratefulness? It's the feelings of thankfulness and appreciation for the physical things, situations and people in our life. Grate-fulness can be expressed in words, emotions, thoughts and actions. What are you grateful for in your life at this moment? What is the first thing that comes to your mind? My first thought was fresh, clean drinking water accessible at all times. We take the simplest things, like clean water, for granted every day, but just take a moment to reflect on how this impacts your life on a daily basis. It would be an enormous challenge to go a day without clean water. I wouldn't even make it through the morning without a cup of coffee. We use water for drinking, cooking, hygiene, cleaning and recreation. Water is not just cleansing and purifying, it also creates and sustains life; we need it for survival. Without drinking water for more than three days, we die. Without water, plants and animals die. My point is that you should take a moment and think of all the things you take for granted on a daily basis that the majority of the world goes without.

I challenge you to practice gratitude throughout the day. Every morning as you open your eyes to embrace a new day, think of something you're grateful for in your life. It can be anything, big or small, just listen to what's in your heart. Smile! You have been gifted with another day to feel joy and bring joy into your life and the lives of others. It starts the day with a sense of wellbeing and completeness as you embrace the possibilities the day may hold. At first this can be challenging, especially if you have been focusing on all the negative aspects of your life. But keep it up, it does get easier and your attitude towards life will start to shift. If you're having a hard time remembering, try placing a note beside your alarm clock as a reminder with the question, 'What am I most grateful for today?' Once you get started, you will soon realise the wonder and beauty that exists in your world. You will find yourself automatically expressing gratitude throughout the day and you will embrace life with new eyes and an open heart.

In order to help you express gratitude in your life, here are some suggestions of things that we often take for granted:

- The roof over your head to protect you from the elements (imagine being in a snow storm and having no shelter or protection!)
- The comfortable bed with pillows and blankets you sleep in at night
- The abundance of clothes and shoes you have for protection and warmth
- The electricity you have, available at a flick of a switch, for heating, lighting, cooking and recreation
- The food you have in your fridge, freezer and pantry to nourish and sustain your life
- The sun in the sky that provides you with warmth, power and life
- Your body, which automatically functions to digest and eliminate waste from your system, keeps your heart beating, creates new cells, fights off invaders using your immune system, processes the air you breathe and repairs your injuries

As you see, I only touched the surface, the list can be almost limitless. When we focus on all the positive things we have in our lives, we will feel content, joy, satisfied and grateful. We tend to overlook the abundance in our everyday lives to focus on the negative aspects. This only gives the negative thoughts more power and a stronger hold to strangle out any joy or hope from our lives.

If you are finding it difficult to be grateful for things in your life, start to dig deeper. What is really holding you back? What life scripts or fears are you hiding from? Why do you feel the need to self-sabotage your own happiness and contentment? Start to journal or meditate on these questions to uncover what's really going on behind the mask. Apply one or more of the essential oils recommended below to help support, nurture and guide you through this journey of self-discovery. Don't be afraid of the unknown or what you might uncover. If you are thinking, Life is just too hard, so why bother? then change that thought to, I am so grateful that I have legs and I can get out of bed or I am grateful for being given the gift of life and I am worth it. Embrace the opportunity to learn, grow and heal. Release what is holding you back and welcome the abundance that is waiting for you. Thank the universe for all the things you do have instead of focusing on what you don't have. You will be amazed at the difference this can make in your life. It starts with one thought at a time; be consistent and the results will be tremendous.

I am grateful for you, the reader, who has inspired me to share my journey and experiences to make a difference one person at a time.

Recommended Essential Oils

- Frankincense
- Helichrysum
- Lavender
- Lime
- Lemongrass
- Myrrh
- Orange
- Peppermint
- Rose
- Sandalwood
- Tangerine

These essential oils can be used singularly or in combinations. Apply 1–3 drops topically on the chest, wrists, back of the neck or bottom of the feet. Inhale directly from the bottle throughout the day as needed or add 1–3 drops to a diffuser.

CHAPTER 9
Manifesting

What do you manifest in your life? It could be a physical disease, unhealthy relationships, limited employment opportunities or a negative attitude. Who and what comes into our lives is a result of what we think about ourselves on a conscious and subconscious level; this is referred to as the laws of attraction. These thoughts come from life scripts that are running in the background that determine our self-worth and beliefs about the world. If you are always thinking the worst is going to happen and putting those thoughts into the universe, they will manifest or reflect back into your life. We will see and experience what we think is the worst that can happen by how we interpret life. If you think you are stupid and can never learn anything new, will you try for that promotion at work? Probably not, you will most likely think and even say that you will never get that job because you're not smart enough. You may even think, Why should I apply? They are not going to give it to a stupid person like me. On the other hand, you could manifest images and attract emotional responses of you sitting at your new desk, performing tasks relating to that new role. Manifest that you are perfect for the role and take steps to prepare for the interview. If called for the interview, you will project confidence and be prepared. Which attitude of the two mentioned above do you think is most likely to apply for the potential promotion?

How do we manifest something we want in our lives? Ask yourself, What do I really want? Be very specific when putting your intentions into the universe. Do you want a more satisfying job in your field of interest that allows your creative talents to blossom? Would you like abundance in finances? What would that look like for you? A six bedroom house with a pool, new sports car or yacht? Maybe you would like to find an intimate partner? If you ask for a man or woman to come into your life, you may get any man or woman. Start visualising the ideal partner you would like in your life. This not only helps the universe know what you want but now you will be more aware of what qualities you are looking for in a partner. Yes, you want someone who will love you, but go deeper. What qualities are important to you in an intimate relationship—great communicator, romantic, respectful, understanding, passionate, caring, spontaneous, generous? What about children, physical attributes and spiritual beliefs? You are putting in your order, so to speak, why leave it to chance?

Now that you have a clear image of what you want to manifest in your life, attach an emotional response to your visualisation. Imagine the emotions and sensations you would be feeling as you sunbathe on the deck of your new yacht. The breeze blowing through your hair, the smell of the salt water and the icy cold fruit smoothie tingling in your mouth. Live out in your mind what you want to manifest in your life as if you already have those things. Your mind can't tell the difference between reality and the reaction happening in your mind and body. It's receiving all the images, impulses and the chemicals reactions attached to your scenario as if it's really happening. As far as your mind and body are concerned, you are on the yacht, cruising along the French Riviera. Now the trick is to repeat this process over and over again in your mind. This will take time and persistence but stick with it. The thoughts and actions you put out into the universe will manifest back into your life. This also goes for your destructive, negative thoughts and actions. Be vigilant and mindful of how powerful your thoughts are, as they will play out in your life in a positive or negative way.

We store past traumas and emotions in our physical bodies. Physical illness and disease is the body manifesting what's happening on an emotional level in our conscious and subconscious mind. Our physical ailments are directly linked to what is going on at the emotional level of an individual. These emotions, traumas, etc. manifest into physical conditions like illness and disease. This is our body's way of saying, 'Hey, look at me. Hello?' It's a warning sign or wakeup call, 'Something is not right here. Are you listening?' There is a mentality in western culture and medicine to mask the symptoms. Buck it up, pop this pill and keep on going; mask what is really going on and what we have manifested.

Have a headache or muscle pain? Just take a pain killer and you won't feel a thing. All better, right? Wrong. That is just another layer of the mask we hide behind, pretending everything is fine. If you take the role of detective and dig deeper into the reasons why you are getting a headache, it will uncover the root cause of your physical afflictions and why it is manifesting physically.

I saw a commercial that showed a mother with a bad cold who was really not in a good way. Red, stuffy nose, headache, fever, etc. you get the point. The commercial was for a cold medicine; just pop this pill and keep on pushing your sick, tired ass because it's expected. Put on the mask that everything is A-OK. Amazing! Now she can take her kids to soccer, bake those cupcakes, go to work and clean the house. All while looking health and happy. This is not only unrealistic but an unhealthy way to respond when we become ill. Again, we are just masking the problem and making it worse.

Another way to look at this cold is as a blessing—your body is letting you know that it has been pushed too far and needs rest to recuperate and regain strength. How about little Tommy misses soccer practice and Mum turns off the oven, calls in sick to work and just lets the house get messy? She needs to put herself first. She should go and lay down to rest and recuperate; that's what her body is telling her it needs. In fact, it really needed it before now. Not listening to the early warning signs made her immune system susceptible to the cold in the first place as it was too weak to fight it off.

Take a look at what going on in your life that's made you susceptible to this illness. What life scripts are running behind the scenes that are affecting how you look after yourself? What treatment is acceptable because of what you feel you deserve? Look at why you are doing this to yourself. It's like a badge of honour that says, 'Look, I am still in control, I have it all together and can do anything.' You don't have to be in control; the world will not fall apart if a soccer game is missed or the kids have cereal for dinner. Respect yourself and your needs. Listen to the warning signs your body is giving you; it's your friend, not your enemy. It may be challenging, but during this time it's okay to ask for help from family and friends. Set the example and have compassion for others by encouraging them to reach out when they are in need.

Start to write down your current illnesses and explore where the root emotional cause could be coming from. I have found throughout my own journey that investigating and openly peeling back the layers of denial has helped open my eyes to the emotional issues I was hiding from. Only you have the power to heal yourself emotionally, physically and spiritually by looking at what you are manifesting in your life. Listed below are some ideas to get you listening to what your body is telling you. For a comprehensive list, I recommend Louise Hay's book, *Heal your Body.* Look at your physical symptoms or illness and ask yourself, How have I manifested this in my life? Be honest with yourself and investigate the root causes of your conditions. Is it an emotional issue that is unresolved? Have you attached yourself to a generational life script that contradicts your true self?

I have included affirmations associated with some physical illness that can manifest in the body. I have found that speaking these affirmations out loud increases their effectiveness; there is real power in verbally proclaiming these affirmations over your life. Using a mirror as you perform these verbal affirmations allows you to stare deep into your eyes, into the depths of your soul and connect with your true self.

Addiction (food, drugs, work, sex, exercise, alcohol) – Slowing killing self, don't deserve to live

- I love and approve of myself
- I am worthy

Anxiety – Doubting and distrusting the flow of life

- I love and trust life is always there for me
- I love and trust myself

Back pain – Fear, distrust life, unsupported

- Life loves and supports me
- I trust life will always support me

Cellulite, body image, body fat – Anger, fear, self-punishment and lack of self-acceptance

- I love, value and appreciate myself
- I am beautiful inside and out
- I accept myself

Circulation – Refusal to go with the flow of life, stagnant

- I trust the process of life
- I am free and flow easily with change

Depression – Guilty for being angry, loss of hope
- I easily release other people's restrictions and limitations
- I am responsible for my life

Digestion process – Find it hard to process life, holding on, not wanting to let go
- I easily let go and flow with change
- I forgive easily and release the past

Female issues – Rejection of feminine side and self
- I embrace my womanhood and love my feminine nature

Inflammation – Irate, the body is physically bursting with anger
- My thoughts are calm, I am peaceful and in control of my thoughts

Knees, feet, hips, legs – Guilt, fear of moving forward in life, stuck
- Life easily flows through me
- I am flexible and free

Neck, throat issues – Not speaking up for self, restricted
- I freely speak up for myself and can see other perspectives to a situation

Pain – Guilt, the need to punishment self
- I easily release the past
- I forgive myself and others

Skin – The need to protect true self
- I freely express myself
- I am safe and free to be me

Tumours – Remorseful about the past
- I easily release the past and welcome the present
- I am safe

Recommended Essential Oils
- Bergamot
- Clary Sage
- Coriander
- Fennel
- Frankincense
- Lemon
- Lemongrass
- Vetiver
- Ylang Ylang

These essential oils can be used singularly or in combinations. Apply 1–3 drops topically on the wrists, stomach, behind the ears or neck. Inhale directly from the bottle throughout the day as needed or add 1–3 drops to a diffuser.

CHAPTER 10

Relationships and Boundaries

D o you finding yourself repeating the same relationship patterns over and over with a different person but the same outcome? Do you always attract the same type of person and situations in life, just a different name and face? It is because you're projecting to others how you feel you deserve to be treated. What little value you place on your self-worth and the repetitive negative life scripts that are running in your life influence how others treat you.

It is a very common story: jumping from one relationship to the next, looking for someone else to make you happy, to complete you, to make you feel loved; always searching for someone else who can change how you feel about yourself. First, you must learn to love *yourself*. These feeling come from within, through self-acceptance and self-love. Until we can cultivate these feeling inwardly, we can never believe or accept love from others. Why, you ask? Because if we can't love ourselves, we can't recognise that someone else can possibly love us. This goes back to life scripts and how we feel about ourselves at a core level. Find out who you are and what makes you happy. Your hopes and dreams, independent of relying on someone else to fulfil those unmet needs in your life. Work on yourself first then you will have the skills and insight to identify a loving, healthy relationship when it comes your way.

Have you ever heard the saying, 'Two halves make a whole' or the expression, 'My other half'? This way of thinking about relationships can be dangerous to how we feel and value ourselves as an individual. Ask yourself, Am I relying on another person to make me feel whole, loved or complete? What happens if they decide to leave the relationship? How would I cope if they left? Relying on someone else for your self-esteem and self-worth is setting yourself up for unnecessary suffering. If you base any percentage of how you feel about yourself on another person's opinion, does this mean they determine how you feel about yourself? Can you control what they say or do? Can you force them to stay because of your own insecurities? Is it not better to feel complete and whole within yourself? A relationship with another person should only enhance your experiences in life. That way if or when a relationship ends, you still feel loved and complete.

Sometimes we can be in a state of denial about what is really going on in our relationship. The false lure of the fairy-tale is so great—that quest for love and the right person who will fix everything and make us happy. We want so badly for this to be true that we ignore or doubt our inner judgement, make excuses or just turn a blind eye. The signs are there but in desperation to find that perfect relationship, our Mr Right, we self-sabotage our own happiness. Unless we address our behaviour patterns that have originated from our life scripts, we will repeat the same relationship patterns over and over.

The mind plays tricks and we block out what we don't want to see in the other person. We convince ourselves they are the one, even when deep down we know they are not the right person. It's time to stand up and break the destructive cycles in your life and be empowered. Ask questions about the other person's motives and how their words or actions really make you feel. Be honest with yourself and connect to your intuition—it is always there to guide and support you. No one deserves to be abused, controlled or belittled by another person, especially under the pretence of love. Life is too short, share your life with people who bring out the best in you, not the worst.

Look at the type of partner you are attracting and if their value system aligns with your own. Under what circumstances has the relationship come about? When a person starts an intimate relationship with a person who is already in another relationship, will they then be surprised when that person cheats on them? We can come up with all kinds of excuses and situations to try and validate why that person is cheating, we may even repeat the justification they used to try and convince us that their behaviour is excusable. They are not in love anymore, they are just together for the kids, they never have sex anymore or there are financial benefits to consider. These are just cop-outs and excuses for not owning their own behaviour and their role in the outcome. However, this does provide a lot of insight about the life scripts running in yourself and the other person's conscious and subconscious mind. That is, of course, if we choose to look at the signs or pretend it will be different in this relationship because you're in love. Well, they most likely felt that way at one point or another with the person they are currently cheating on. They will cheat on a partner, lie, deceive, shift the blame and lack communication skills. Unless they honestly look at their behaviour, they are most likely going to repeat the same pattern of behaviour. Basically, if we don't change our behaviours or thought patterns, how can we expect the outcome of our relationships to be any different? What is the definition of insanity? Doing the same thing over and over expecting a different result. I know it's simple but sometimes the simplest things can be clouded by our emotions and fear of looking inward, to face the truth. Facing the truth is liberating, free and healing, because it allows you to let go of your false self. Only you can free yourself from repeating the same negative relationship patterns by valuing and respecting yourself.

The types of relationship you allow in your life mirror how you feel about yourself and what you feel you deserve. Love yourself first or it will be hard to accept love from others because the concept is foreign. If we have never loved ourselves, we find it hard that someone would love us as we view ourselves as unworthy of love or unlovable. Positive relationships are based on communication, mutual respect and compromise. Don't expect someone to read your mind—communicate your needs and how you are feeling. In turn, be open to listen to what the other person in the relationship needs. The importance of positive, open communication cannot be over-stated in a healthy relationship. How can the other person know what you feel or need if you don't communicate this information?

Negative relationships can manifest from control, disrespect and poor communication. Take a look at who you spend your time with, whether it's an intimate relationship with a partner, family member, co-worker, community member or friend. Start looking at how you interact with each other. How do they make you feel about yourself after you have spent time together? Do you feel drained and negative or uplifted and energised? Journaling what you discover about the types of relationship in your life will help you have a greater understanding of the life scripts that are playing out in your life. The key is to look at them as if they are out of balance and how they make you feel. For example, in a healthy relationship, there is compromise and roles switch back and forth. You may be having a bad day and need support from the other person but next week they might need similar support from you. It's when the behaviours are controlling, manipulative, all one-sided and degrading that the red flags need to be addressed.

Here are some suggestions to give you an idea of how to evaluate different types of negative relationship patterns:

- Always taking from others, using them
- Talking about others in a negative manner
- Manipulative tactics
- Trying to control others for personal gain or power
- Degrading or putting others down
- Always negative
- Disrespectful
- Untrustworthy, lying

Boundaries

Boundaries can be physical and energetic. Physical boundaries refer to your physical location and your personal space. Energetic boundaries also exist in physical space but mostly refer to the energies exchanged between people and places. We can physically remove ourselves from a situation; move out of the household, resign from our employer or decline hanging out with another person. This will also influence and lessen their negative energetic effect towards us. Energetic vampires and parasites emotionally and physically drain our energy and resources, leaving us open for an attack. Throughout my own journey, I have noticed that when my energy is weak or I have been sick, it attracts abusers back into my life. During these times, I needed to be more vigilant because it's easy to slip back into old life scripts and destructive behaviour patterns. It's like the predator that senses your weakness and goes in for the attack. Even when we remove ourselves and put boundaries in place with another person, we can relive it in our minds over and over. By constantly reliving the situation in our mind, have we really freed ourselves from misery? By being in that mind space, we are still emotionally attached to that situation. The body continues to feed off these hormonal responses like a drug addict getting their fix. Clear your mind through mediation practices and detach from the wild emotional rollercoaster you have created.

Now this is the touchy subject for some people: What about family? You can't pick them so how do you deal with them in a positive manner? Just note that it's not okay for anyone to disrespect, control or physically or verbally abuse another person, even if they are related. We can't and shouldn't try to control other people's behaviour or try to force them to change; it needs to come from their willingness to change. It's a trap to think, Oh, I can change that person. I have had to end relationships with certain members of my own family. If a person puts you down, belittles you and makes you feel bad about yourself, how do you think that's going to work out for you emotionally? I'm not saying you should disown your family but put boundaries in place regarding what kind of behaviour is acceptable; then it's their choice whether they want to respect you or not. You can still love them, but it does not mean you have to include them in your life if they treat you poorly. Wrap them in love and send them on their way! If and when they respect your boundaries, welcome them back with love, forgiveness and encouragement.

Your personal power is your birthright and only you can willingly give it away to another person. Giving up your personal power is a way of self-punishing or allowing others to control, punish and abuse you because of life scripts running in your life.

No one should ever try to control another person; it's degrading and disrespectful, not to mention very destructive. If someone in your life is disrespectful or controlling, it's because you allow them to be that way in the first place. These self-beliefs and behaviour patterns can become so ingrained in us that they operate on auto-pilot through our subconscious. We can be unaware and in a state of denial because it's too difficult to face, especially when you have been in this situation for a considerable amount of time. It can feel hopeless, as if there is no light at the end of the tunnel. Don't ever give your personal power away to anyone for any reason. This does not mean you can't trust another person but by knowing yourself you can identify when someone is trying to disrespect your boundaries. If someone is trying to take your personal power, they do not have your best interest at heart, nor do they respect you as a person. Run like hell!

If someone says they can't live without you or are going to kill themselves if you leave, you cannot help them by staying; you are only enabling their behaviour. There was probably major underlying problems for that person to begin with and the relationship has only brought them to a breaking point. Ask yourself, Are things going to change? Look at why you might be staying. Do you feel guilty that their death will be on your hands if you leave? Don't; it is *their* choice. Is it because you don't feel like you deserve any better treatment? This is a false life script running behind the scenes in your mind. Is it the ego saying, 'It sure feels good to be loved that much'? Is it your desire to be their rescuer, whether they want to be saved or not? Are you fearful of being alone or feel that no one else will want you or you will feel rejected?

These are just some clues as to what could be behind your motivation for having this detrimental relationship in your life. Always question your behaviour and look at patterns. Journaling your progress can reveal patterns that you're trying to hide from yourself. Allow them to come to the light so you can move towards awareness and healing. You can only see clearly through taking an honest look at your thoughts and behaviours, dealing with your emotional issues and setting yourself free from misery. By taking the time to identify your behaviour patterns and making positive changes, you can have positive, rewarding relationships.

Recommended Essential Oils

- Cinnamon
- Cilantro
- Clove
- Eucalyptus
- Fennel
- Geranium
- Lavender
- Marjoram
- Melaleuca
- Rose
- Rosemary

These essential oils can be used singularly or in combinations. Apply 1–3 drops topically on the chest, stomach, back of the neck or bottom of the feet. Inhale directly from the bottle throughout the day as needed or add 1–3 drops to a diffuser.

CHAPTER 11

Live In the Moment

Too often we spend more time reliving the past or worrying about the future than living in the present moment. How are you meant to live life if you're not really mentally present? Instead, you are racing around in your mind, repeating a continuous loop of the same information. By doing this, we miss out on life; what is happening all around us, every second of every day. Ask yourself, How is repeatedly replaying the past benefiting me? What is the point in obsessively thinking about past events that can't be altered, or worrying about future events that can't be predicted? Question yourself. Is it out of fear, guilt, regret, hatred, betrayal or shame? Be honest with yourself and what emotions come up during this process. This is the only way to get to the root cause of your thought and behaviour patterns.

Your thoughts determine what actions you take in life, which in turn determines your reality. If you continue to look back at the closed doors of the past, you will miss the new doors opening in the present. Think of all the wasted energy and emotional distress caused by living and thinking in this mindset. Just imagine if you put that energy into living in the present with new thoughts that supported you and made you feel good about yourself and the world. It's time to break free from the chains of the past and start living your life in the present. Open yourself up to what is happening right now. Look around, what do you see, feel, hear, smell and taste? Use all your senses to soak in life and focus on what you are grateful for right now.

Sometime we can fall into the trap of looking forward to something so much that we can spend countless amounts of time thinking about the event before it even happens. When the event finally takes place, it is almost impossible to live up to the expectations we created in our mind beforehand. We end up feeling disappointed and let down by the experience because it did not match our expectations. We even miss out on fully enjoying the present experience. Instead, we spend time comparing the reality of the present moment with the scenarios created in our mind before the event. How can we be fully immersed when our mind keeps jumping back and forth from stored memories to the present? This is not even taking into account that our mind is also running wild with other past repeated thought patterns. In the past, I have even started planning my next holiday while on holiday. I had already taken the holiday in my mind long before I even embarked on the trip. I was already living in the future, totally missing out on my present adventure.

One of my friends shared with me a profound moment in his life. He was working outside as an excavator, lost in thoughts that had been replaying hundreds of times in his mind about past regrets and fear of the future. His work colleague said, 'Hey, check this out.' He immediately felt anger rising up inside and thought, What are you bugging me for? Then he looked up. The most amazingly beautiful sunset was happening right before his eyes. He was oblivious to the wonder happening around him because he was living out the past and the future in his mind. This was a life-changing moment for him as he became aware of his negative thought patterns and how they were affecting his life. He realised by living in the past and future, he was missing out on what was really important—the present.

Living in the Present Moment Challenge

The next time you are doing a mundane task—washing the dishes, hanging up the laundry, watering the garden—fully immerse yourself in what you are doing; the here and now. Let's take a look at watering the garden as an example of how to perform this exercise. Clear your mind of everything except the task at hand. In your mind, walk yourself through every tiny action you're completing while watering the garden. Start with thinking, I am walking to the tap, the ground feels dry under my feet. I am turning the handle to the tap, it feels cool to the touch and I can hear the water flowing through the hose. Mindfully take in everything that you're smelling, seeing, hearing, touching and tasting. Engage all five of your senses. Watch the water flow from the hose onto the leaves of the plants; see how it trickles down to the earth. Notice the colours and the different shades of the rainbow made from the water spray as it reflects the light. Inhale the fragrance of your herbs or flowers. Take notice of what emotions arise from the scents and your experience. As you harvest and taste a snow pea, feel the smooth shell and listen to the crisp snap as you take a bite. Touch the water as it flows, feel the coolness and have gratitude for its life-giving nourishment.

This exercise not only helps you live in the moment but also clears your mind of that endless chatter and negative repetitive thought patterns about the past and the future. This is a form of mediation and can help you train your mind to become more focused. By actively focusing on your thought patterns, it increases your awareness, allowing you to have more control over your thoughts.

As discussed earlier, our thoughts become our actions. We can blindly go through our lives at the whim and volatility of our emotions or we can have a clear perspective of reality without the emotional attachments. Take ownership of the role you play in the outcomes in your life. We are not just bystanders in the journey of life but can experience its abundance by living in the present moment. What a liberating experience to know that, with practice, we can live to our full potential by adjusting our thoughts. What do you think?

Recommended Essential Oils

- Bergamot
- Cypress
- Ginger
- Grapefruit
- Lemon
- Lime
- Orange
- Tangerine

These essential oils can be used singularly or in combinations. Apply 1–3 drops topically on the wrists, behind the ears, stomach or bottom of the feet. Inhale directly from the bottle throughout the day as needed or add 1–3 drops to a diffuser.

CHAPTER 12
Journal

Journaling is the great way to freely express how we are feeling, free of judgement from others, constraints and restrictions. It provides the opportunity to explore our thought patterns and behaviours in a safe environment. Have you ever felt like there was so much information racing around in your head it might explode? Or felt that your mind was all jumbled up, as if your thoughts and emotions were jumping around like jack rabbits? Or the ever so familiar repetition of the same information over and over and over like a broken record?

Journaling can assist you in breaking free from these unhealthy thought patterns by helping you to acknowledge the information, reflect on what's driving the behaviour and think about how you can process that information in a productive manner. Journal based on your feeling and emotions; no judgement, no criticism, just explore. Think of it as an exciting adventure. If you have never journaled before or are finding it difficult to begin, just start by writing about anything. For example, what you did during the day or what your plans are for the weekend. This will help you get used to expressing your feelings through writing.

What You Will Need to Get Started:

- An open mind
- A journal
- A pen
- Essential oils
- A quiet place

Find your own special place where you feel safe, comfortable and secure. My preferred spot is on the veranda, overlooking the mountains, where I can immerse myself in all the beauty of nature. This allows me to have a clearer perspective and a feeling of gratitude as I begin my inward journey. Next, apply essential oils topically, inhale directly from the bottle or use a diffuser in the room.

Sometimes it can be difficult to express ourselves during the journaling process because of our life scripts and experiences. This can also manifest with our throats tightening up or not being able to speak up for ourselves in intimate or public settings. Lavender is a useful essential oil in this situation as it supports the body by calming fears, specifically for the throat, giving us courage and strength to regain our voice and express ourselves freely. Apply 1–2 drops of lavender essential oil on the throat area.

With pen in hand, start by asking yourself questions about one of the thought patterns or life scripts you identified in earlier chapters. Write down the thought, for example, Fear of the future. What is it that you fear? Death? Being alone? Getting cancer? Ask yourself, Is this fear real or have I convinced myself with endless scenarios that this will manifest in my life? Reflect on what is really driving your emotional responses. Now that you are aware of some of your thought patterns, what's next? Be a detective, keep digging and asking questions. Asking yourself questions like, Why do I feel this way? Refer to the emotions chart in Chapter 4 to help identify and explore your true emotions at a deeper level. Think of patterns in your own life as well as generational patterns in your family. It's time to break the destructive cycles in your life and move forward with love and joy.

Free flow with your journaling. If you start to feel emotions stirring, begin to tear up or become flushed, you are hitting a spot that needs emotional work. Keep probing and asking questions because you have hit a nerve. It is your choice to dig deeper or reject this emotional healing opportunity. If you choose to avoid this area and let your mind go off in another direction, be aware that this issue will keep coming up over and over, until you deal with it or it manifests into disease. This is a point to re-centre your focus and ask yourself, What am I hiding from? Only you can take this journey of emotional healing and explore your true self.

Your journal can be used to write a letter to a person who has hurt you in the past or if unresolved issues remain. This is your opportunity to have a voice and say all the things that you have held inside for so long. The letters are not intended to go to the other person, so look within and be honest about how you feel. Sometimes it's hard to admit to ourselves that we have been betrayed or abandoned. This is your opportunity to acknowledge how you feel, reflect and process your emotions. When you let go of the past and forgive yourself and others, you are free to live life.

The first letter you write may be to the other person, expressing how you feel about the situation. Next, write a letter to yourself responding to the first letter as the other person. This process is continued back and forth until you're satisfied that the issues are resolved. Remember, we all have our own stories and experiences that shape the way we behaviour towards others. It's impossible to know what someone is dealing with behind their mask or imagine the traumas they have endured. Looking at it from this perspective helps us connect with the other person through empathy, compassion and forgiveness.

Performing a burning ceremony of journals or letters can also be cathartic in the healing process. It symbolises a letting go of the past and moving forward with forgiveness in your heart. Ceremonies and rituals have been a part of our ancestry. They provide a spiritual connection to the universe and a physical release of emotions. It's unbeneficial to stir up past traumatic events without processing and releasing these repressed feelings. Burning diary entries or letters can be part of the process of letting go and allowing yourself to feel closure. Watching the smoke float into the sky symbolises a release to the universe. Speak aloud your intention of forgiveness and release yourself and the other person. Allow both of you to be free and move forward. Leaving the past opens up a future by living in the present.

In my own journey, I found journaling empowering and healing when working through my experiences of sexual abuse. I have reread old journals that I had written years ago during a time when I felt hopeless, consumed in anger, fear, denial and resentment; spinning out of control in circles of confusion and misery. Reading about how I was coping and dealing with situations and people was an empowering and encouraging experience. Reflecting back on those hard times made me so grateful that I chose the path of emotional healing. It has been challenging and difficult but worth more than words can express. My tears now come from joy—yes, joy! Can you imagine that this life is possible for you? It is yours for the taking if you choose love over fear. What will you choose?

Recommended Essential Oils

- Black Pepper
- Cilantro
- Clary Sage
- Fennel
- Frankincense
- Helichrysum
- Lavender
- Melissa
- Rosemary
- Ylang Ylang

These essential oils can be used singularly or in combinations. Apply 1–3 drops topically on the wrists, behind the ears or bottom of the feet. Inhale directly from the bottle throughout the day as needed or add 1–3 drops to a diffuser.

CHAPTER 13

Mirror, Mirror on the Wall

What is mirror work? Mirror work is looking at yourself in a mirror and speaking affirmations over your life. Mirror work is a totally different way of looking at yourself and connecting inward. By looking directly at your face and eyes it creates a deep connection; a link to your true self. Your eyes are the windows into your soul. This exercise can be powerful and confronting. The first time I experienced mirror work was in one of my early counselling session. I was unable to look in the mirror without crying out of control. I hated myself so much; I was ashamed and disgusted. Who was this person in the mirror? I did not even recognise who I had become, this distorted image I had created of myself. I dare not look, I was overcome with fear and anxiety. Looking back at my first experience, I am amazed at my reaction. I had been looking in the mirror every day of my life—brushing my teeth, combing my hair, putting on makeup—but this was different. This was facing my pain, fear, torment, self-loathing and shame; confronting all the false beliefs and walls I had built around me for protection. My fortress was under attack; 'all hands on deck'. My counsellor didn't push this technique at the time and focused on building my self-worth in other ways.

It was not till years later on my own that I picked up the mirror again for the purpose of emotional healing. I was ready to face what was behind the walls; behind the false mask of illusion. I started with the simple affirmation, 'I love you.' My approach was as an observer with an open heart, ready to accept love into my life. This technique had quick and profound effects on my life and how I felt about myself. By affirming the love I have for myself, it created a domino effect in my life and the way I felt about myself. I wanted to heal emotionally and physically because I now felt worth it, loved, respected and accepted. It helped me rediscover my self-worth and embrace the beauty within all of us. I continue the practice of mirror work on a daily basis. Okay, I do miss a day here or there, but that's okay, it's about living life out of love not punishment. Don't beat yourself up, have compassion, empathy and forgiveness for yourself. Rejoice in your accomplishments instead of focusing on the negatives, because what's the point in that? It will only make you feel bad about yourself. Is that the life you want to choose?

No time like the present—let's get started! The first affirmation I suggest starting out with for mirror work is 'I love you'. To me, this sets the basis for how you feel about yourself. Learning to fully love yourself opens your heart to seeking out what is best for you in all areas of life. It's the foundations of self-respect and self-worth; knowing that you desire and deserve a better life for yourself. Have fun with the mirror. Watch a young child; how do they act in front of a mirror? They have fun; exploring, laughing, making faces. Embrace your youthful heart, sing the affirmations, blow yourself a kiss in the mirror or have a heart to heart with yourself. Don't take yourself too seriously; smile and have fun.

'I Love You' Affirmation

Centre yourself and take a few belly breathes to calm your mind and body. Belly breathing is inhaling air into the lower stomach only and keeping your chest from raising. It can be helpful to put on hand on your stomach and the other hand on your chest. This type of breathing send signals to your brain relaying you are safe and calm. Start with the mirror about a foot from your face. First look into your left eye and repeat the affirmation, 'I love you, (insert name). I love you'. Next, look into your right eye and repeat the same affirmation, 'I love you, (insert name). I love you'. Finally, draw the mirror away from your face, at about arm's length, and look into both eyes. Taking in the whole face, repeat the same affirmation, 'I love you, (insert name). I love you'.

Repeat this affirmation first thing in the morning and before you go to bed at night. If possible, try several times during the day using a bathroom mirror or your cell phone reflection. The more times you say this powerful affirmation over your life, the quicker you will replace old negative life scripts with your newfound self-love. Try this for several weeks and reflect on your emotions during this practice. It can be helpful to journal about these emotions as a way of exploring hidden life scripts or repressed memories.

Working with a mirror can be challenging and confronting. If you're having difficulty at first, don't be discouraged. Take a few deep breaths, followed by belly breathing as a way to calm and centre your being. Continue with the belly breathing throughout the affirmation exercise. When you feel calm and centred, hold the mirror at arm's length from your face. Repeat the affirmation, 'I am willing to try and love myself today. I am open to accepting self-love'. Repeat this affirmation while looking at yourself in the mirror for two more times if possible. Respect how you are feeling and be mindful not to let fear control your ability to love.

If you are finding looking in the mirror too confronting, think of flexible solutions—other ways of accomplishing the task at hand. Try visualising your eyes or face and repeat, 'I love you' either out loud or in your mind. It's easy to think of excuses and self-sabotage when we are confronting our false belief system. We cling so desperately to the very things that make us feel hopeless and miserable, out of fear and false comfort. You can break free from the chains of suffering. It's all about choices and consequences for our actions. Only you can instigate change over your life, good or bad. The power is yours, stand up and shine!

The list below contains some suggested affirmations for you to try. Simply use the instructions from the 'I love you' affirmation and insert the affirmation of your choice.

List of Affirmations

- I love you, (insert your name)
- I am safe, secure and supported
- I am supported by the universe
- Life always provides for all my needs in abundant ways
- I love life and embrace its magnificence
- I release the old and welcome the new
- I embrace change with ease
- I easily forgive myself and others
- My life is full of abundance in all areas
- My life is flexible, free and flowing
- I forgive myself and others
- I find change easily flows through me on all levels
- I release thoughts of anger
- I trust life always supports me
- I am open to loving others and myself
- I trust myself and my intuition
- The possibilities in life are limitless
- I am surrounded by love

- I cherish and comfort myself
- I lovingly embrace my intuition and all its gifts
- I approve of myself and others
- I make my own rules that support me in positive ways
- My life is always going in the best direction
- My thoughts are loving and calm

Recommend Essential Oils

- Black Pepper
- Bergamot
- Cassia
- Cilantro
- Cypress
- Frankincense
- Rosemary
- Wintergreen
- Ylang Ylang

These essential oils can be used singularly or in combinations. Apply 1–3 drops topically on the wrists, behind the ears or bottom of the feet. Inhale directly from the bottle throughout the day as needed or add 1–3 drops to a diffuser.

CHAPTER 14

Filling Your Tank

Giving to others and helping others should bring love, satisfaction and fulfilment. When you are out of balance, you feel resentment, unappreciated or used. We tend to show generosity towards other people because it mirrors how we want to be treated in our own life. When we give to others and neglect ourselves physically and emotionally, our tank becomes empty. Picture this, you only have so many resources and so much energy. Now take some out for work, running the household, relationships, kids, giving to others; the list can really feel endless at times as your tank gets lower and lower.

If you look at all the things we do in life, they either fill our tanks or empty our tanks. When you put the needs of others ahead of your own and rarely (or never) fill up your own tank, it will run empty. This will cause you to feel constantly tired, hopeless, angry, short-tempered and unappreciated. We can't help others in a healthy way unless we help ourselves first. I know society and certain religions promote the idea that we should always help others and put others first; so much so that we are placed at the bottom of the totem pole. But isn't this an unrealistic way to function physically and emotionally? Putting yourself first does not make you selfish or conceited. On the contrary, it helps you ensure that you always have the resources and energy to help others from a place of love and joy, not obligation.

I fell into the trap of helping others and neglecting myself. I did this for a few reasons; the main reason was to help people. I truly believe part of my journey on earth is to share my knowledge and help others. Out of false beliefs and self-hatred, combined with an abusive relationship, helping others manifested in negative ways in my life. I was in such a deep state of denial about the situations I was in and tried at all costs not to deal with it on an emotional level. I was always helping others, being the 'perfect' mother, the 'perfect' wife and the 'perfect' little helper. The strategy at the time, even though I did not acknowledge it, was to keep as busy as possible. This way I did not have to deal with my own emotional issues. To the outside world, my false mask—my false self—looked like I was A-OK; helping others, working and taking care of my family. Inside, I was slowly dying, bit by bit, until my body said, 'Enough, I want to live!' That's when my depression dropped me to my knees, literally. I was on one of my usual walks and—bang!—it felt like I was going to die of a blood clot or something. The pain in my head was so intense I had to lie down beside the dirt road, wondering if I was going to die. My energy levels quickly depleted to the point that walking up a flight of fifteen stairs meant stopping two or three times as I pulled myself up by the hand rails. I was physically forced to sit down and be with my thoughts. At first I tried so hard to fight against myself. I would sit there crying, wanting to get up and pull that weed or pick up that toy, grasping to keep my world together; anything to stop the wall from crumbling down so I could carry on my 'everything is perfect' facade.

These days, I put myself first and make sure my tank is full. That way, I have the resources to help others out of love and compassion. Now I am able to say no without having to give a reason or justify that I need to take care of myself. I am worth it—my health and emotional wellbeing is worth it. You are worth it too!

What truly makes you happy? I know at one point in my life, I could not answer that question. We can become so disconnected from our true self that we can feel like a stranger in our own skin. Think back to when you were a child. What made you smile or brought you joy? For me, it was animals, flowers, being in nature, swinging, laughing and dancing. Just because we grow up, it does not mean that we can't enjoy things in life with the enthusiasm of a child. This nurtures our inner child and fills our tank with abundance and joy. It triggers creativity and stimulates the right side of the brain, which is responsible for emotion, imagination, music, instinct, art and memory. In contrast, the left side of the brain is the logical side, which is responsible for rational, objective, analytic and digital thinking. We need both sides to function but, as with everything, balance is the thread of the universe. The Chinese refer to this as yin and yang. It is light and darkness; hot and cold.

Here are some suggestions that might help you fill your tank. If you're not sure what you like to do, think back to what has brought you joy and happiness throughout your life. For fun, why not try something new that you always wanted to do. It can be eye-opening to make a list of the things that make you happy. Next make a list of the things you do every day. Compare both lists and adjust accordingly.

- Watch a sunset
- Read a book
- Take a walk
- Sky dive
- Watch the clouds
- Go for a swim
- Meditate
- Walk on the beach
- Write in a journal
- Visit a friend
- Volunteer
- Ride a bike
- Dance
- Cook your favourite meal
- Take a class
- Play music

- Create
- Grow a garden
- Pet an animal
- Take a nap
- Live in the moment
- Yoga
- Get a massage
- Sew
- Watch an inspirational movie
- Breathe
- Paint a picture
- Aromatherapy
- Laugh
- Be grateful
- Bungie jump
- Picnic in the park
- Photography
- Walk in a garden
- Listen to live music
- Paddle boarding
- Go on holiday
- Join a group
- Climb a mountain
- Learn a foreign language
- Read or write poetry
- Hug yourself and others
- Colour a picture
- Body relaxation techniques
- Soak in a bath
- Sing like no one is listening
- Visit a museum or art gallery

Recommended Essential Oils

- Cedarwood
- Coriander
- Cypress
- Lemon
- Lime
- Orange
- Peppermint
- Rose
- Tangerine
- White Fir
- Ylang Ylang

These essential oils can be used singularly or in combinations. Apply 1–3 drops topically on the stomach or bottom of the feet. Inhale directly from the bottle throughout the day as needed or add 1–3 drops to a diffuser.

CHAPTER 15
Why Meditate?

Meditation is not about going to la-la-land and having an empty mind. It's focused, internal concentration. Focus on your breath, a thought, a concept or energy. If we allow our minds to run like a wild monkey with no control over our thoughts, we will remain unfocused and at the mercy of our emotions. You may think, *That's just the way my mind works.* I recall once, in a moment of desperation, I just wanted all the internal noise to *stop!* My mind would relentlessly repeat over and over and over the same situations with no other outcome than to drive me mad. The thought patterns were negative, destructive, counterproductive and a major energy zapper. I would wallow around in my own misery with no clue or awareness there was another way to think, another way to live. Meditation allows the monkey mind to settle down and increases our ability to see things clearly. This way we can objectively look at our thought patterns and see past our delusions. It assists in revealing unhealthy behaviour patterns that are detrimental to our wellbeing. We can have control over what we think, which in turn creates our world. If you choose to have repeated negative thoughts, negativity will manifest in your life. If you choose to have repeated positive thoughts, positivity will manifest in your life. It's the basic universal law of attraction. What we put out into the universe is what we will get back from the universe.

Meditation is about training your brain and like any muscle in the body, it takes time to condition. At first it will be difficult to remain focused but don't be discouraged. Any amount of time should be viewed as an accomplishment, even if it's only a few seconds. Rejoice in your accomplishment instead of beating yourself up; this is an example of looking at a situation in a positive light.

Be mindful not to self-sabotage—that is only a convenient cop-out that will halt your healing. When you start any new activity, it takes time and practice. When you find your mind slipping to what's on the shopping list or a negative thought—which it will—acknowledge the thought and visualise it drifting away like grains of sand in a gentle breeze. With practice, you will be able to stay focused on your meditation for longer periods of time. Your mind will slip back to unproductive or unhealthy thoughts some days more than others. That's okay; have empathy and compassion for your situation or how you may be feeling in that moment. The sooner we accept we are not perfect, the sooner we can live and enjoy life to the fullest without restrictions.

What You Will Need to Get Started:

- An open mind
- A quiet place
- A chair or mat
- A pillow or folded blanket
- Essential oils

I use the following techniques as they work well for me. We are all different so do what feels right for you, go for it, relax and don't take yourself too seriously. First, find a quiet place to sit down either on the floor or a chair; lying down is usually not suggested because it can bring about sleepiness and loss of focus. Ultimately, do what feels right for your body; if you're uncomfortable then that is what you will focus on, taking away from the meditation. Next, apply, inhale or diffuse 1–3 drops of essential oils to enhance your experience and healing potential. Place a pillow or folded blanket on the mat. The object is to have your hips higher than your legs while in a seated position. Sit with your legs in a crossed position, referred to as the half lotus posture. This is accomplished by placing one foot on the opposite thigh while the other foot rests under the other thigh. If this is uncomfortable, adjust by crossing your legs with your feet on the floor. Next, place your right hand on top of the left in your lap with your palms facing up. Another alternative is resting one hand on each knee with the palms facing down. Relax your shoulders down away from your ears. Open up the chest area to allow your breath to flow freely and naturally. Now bring focus to your spine. Imagine your spine is a straight line from the lower back all the way to the top of your head. Tucking your chin in slightly to the throat will assist with aligning your spine correctly. Gently place the tip of the tongue on the roof of your mouth near the front teeth. Your eyes can be half shut or fully open, depending on how you are feeling. If you are nervous, excited or anxious, have your eyes half closed; if you are feeling tired, lethargic or have low energy, have your eyes fully open. Remember to modify your posture to suit what works for you and your body. The above is just a guideline to help you to get started on your meditation journey.

Clear your mind of what you plan on cooking for dinner or the laundry that needs doing. Acknowledge these thoughts but instead of holding on to them, release them like grains of sand, gently blowing away in the breeze. Follow your breath, feeling the air flow through your nostrils, filling your lungs. Notice the temperature of your breath and feel yourself settle into the natural rhythm.

Described above is the preparation for any meditation and can be continued in different directions. The following are a few examples of mediations to help get you started:

Altruistic Love (Loving Kindness)

I visualise a blonde-haired young child, around a year old, smiling as they come toward me. As they approach, I gently brush their hair back from their smiling face and think of altruistic love. I start to feel this love fill my body, usually along the spine and out the top of my head. My body is then engulfed in a feeling a love, comfort, warmth and belonging. I soak it up, basking in this pure love energy. Then I begin to share it with the world, starting on a personal level. I start by sending altruistic love to my friends and family; I may name individual people or areas, it depends on what is on my heart at the time.

Then—this is the challenging part but it does get easier with forgiveness—I send altruistic love to the people that have hurt me in my life. When I first started incorporating this into my meditation, the feeling of altruistic love depleted at a rapid rate when focusing this energy towards those individuals. When this happened, I would visualise the small child again, build up the love energy and focus it back to the person that had treated me poorly. I would then extend altruistic love to the whole world, wrapping it in a big ball of light, extending it throughout all levels of the universe. As always, I bring the altruistic love back to myself.

Slowly bring your awareness back. Circle your wrists, ankles and open your eyes. Observe how you feel physically and emotionally.

Breathing

Position your body and settle into the natural rhythm of your breath, as explained above. This meditation assists in clearing the mind and oxygenating the body. As you breathe in and out through your nose, notice the temperate of your breath. How the air feels flowing in and out of your nostrils. On your next inhale, start to count as you expand the lungs, filling the chest. As you count to four, feel the air fill your lower, middle and upper chest. As you exhale, slowly release the breath while counting to four. Continue to repeat this breathing technique while increasing the numbered count per inhalation and exhalation. Increase to a number that is comfortable and continue with this count for five minutes.

Let go of the controlled breathing and allow your breath to find its natural rhythm. Observe how you feel physically and emotionally.

Focus on an Object

During the setup of the mat and pillow, place a candle or an object a couple of feet in front of your mat. Position your body and settle into the natural rhythm of your breath, as explained above. Next, start to focus your attention on the flame of the candle. Observe how the flame moves and sways. Notice the colours of the flame and how they change. The dancing colours of red, yellow, blue and white. As your focus becomes more concentrated on the candle, the space around the room can become blurred and darker. Let the pure rays of white light radiate from the candle to shower you with love and light.

When you are ready, start to bring your awareness back. Notice how you feel physically and emotionally. Is your mind clearer? Your body more relaxed?

Fear to Safety

This meditation is helpful to counteract feelings of fear and insecurity in yourself or the world. Position your body and settle into the natural rhythm of your breath, as explained above. Visualise yourself in a place where you feel safe. If you feel unsafe everywhere, imagine a place where you would feel safe. Cultivate emotional feelings of safety by attaching an emotional response that triggers your brain into thinking you are safe. Wrap yourself in a ball of white light that encompasses your feelings of safety. Now you are ready to imagine yourself gliding around the room, protected by your ball of light.

Next, visualise yourself going outside, driving the car and going into town. While in your protected white ball of light, go anywhere in the world, do anything; you are safe and secure. After you have experienced the world, bring your awareness back to the heart and rest in the feeling of safety you have created.

The wonderful thing about meditation is that we can tap into these feelings we have created at any time throughout our daily life. We have stored this visual experience of safety in our minds and have attached to it an emotional response. When you are feeling fearful or insecure, just call on your memories of safety from this meditation.

Suggestions for Mediation Topics

- Anger to love
- Forgiveness of yourself and others
- Altruistic love
- Self-acceptance
- Addiction to release
- Fear to safety
- Self-awareness and body image
- Compassion
- Connection with the universe
- Abundance
- Gratefulness
- Releasing the past
- Empathy

- Breath
- Awareness of physical body
- Focus on an object

Recommended Essential Oils

- Cedarwood
- Clary Sage
- Frankincense
- Lavender
- Melissa
- Patchouli
- Roman Chamomile
- Sandalwood
- Vetiver

For topical application, apply 1–3 drops to wrists and/or back of the neck. Inhale directly from the bottle or add 1–3 drops to a diffuser.

These essential oils can be used singularly or in combinations. I have listed some blends that may be helpful but experiment with what combinations work best for you.

Blend 1

- 1 drop cedarwood
- 1 drop lavender
- 1 drop patchouli

Blend 2

- 1 drop frankincense
- 1 drop clary sage
- 1 drop melissa

Blend 3

- 1 drop sandalwood
- 1 drop lavender
- 1 drop vetiver

CHAPTER 16

Body Relaxation Technique

The body relaxation technique is a beautiful way to reconnect with yourself and melt away any tension, stored trauma or stress your mind and body are holding on to.

When a bison escapes being eaten to death by a lion and the threat is gone, it does something cathartic. The bison will go find a quiet spot under a tree, lie down and release all the built up tension stored in its body from the attack. Its body will shake and shutter, then relax, recovering from the traumatic event. As humans, we seem to ignore this key part in the recovery process. I know we're not getting attacked by loins or other wild animal anymore but in modern society we are still being threatened in others ways that kick our bodies into the flight or fight response. When you get in an argument with your partner, aggressive work colleague or any other form of conflict, the same hormones go coursing through our systems. This is the same survival strategies our ancestors have used for thousands of years. Because our bodies can't process the difference, this automatic response mechanism signals our hormones to start producing.

You may be asking yourself, What happens then? We hold all this tension—this energy—in our bodies until we can release it. If we continue in this state of distress, illness and disease will most likely follow. The body relaxation technique can help the body heal itself quicker and will also boost the immune system. This calm, relaxed state helps to release tension in the body and increases the hormones that promote a sense of wellbeing. When we take time to consciously relax our mind and body, it often brings everything into perspective.

What You Will Need to Get Started:

- A quiet place
- A mat or bed
- A pillow or blanket
- Essential oils

Find a quiet place to begin your relaxation practice. Make this place your own little sanctuary; light a candle, diffuse or apply essential oils or turn down the lights. I recommended doing this technique in a lying down position as your muscles and mind can fully release. A bed or a yoga mat on the floor can help you to feel more comfortable during this exercise. If this is not possible, a sitting position can bring favourable results as well. If you find your back becomes sore, place a pillow under your knees, as this will take the pressure off your lower back. Additionally, if your neck is in an awkward position, place a pillow under your head to help keep your spine in alignment. Place your hands beside your body with the palms facing up. It's all about being comfortable and relaxed; it's all about you letting go.

Start with focusing on your breaths by expanding only the lower part of your stomach; this is known as belly breathing. This type of breathing relays signals to the brain that you are in a calm and relaxed state. Start to feel your heart rate lower as your body releases tension and enters a state of relaxation. This breathing technique can be used anytime, anywhere to help alleviate anxiety and stress.

Begin with your face. In your mind, tell that area to relax and visualise the muscles in your face relaxing. Next, move down to your neck and shoulders. In your mind, tell that area to relax and visualise the muscles in your neck and shoulders relaxing. Move to the arms. In your mind, tell that area to relax and visualise the muscles in your arms relaxing. Follow this same technique through your body: the front torso, legs, back and head. Finally, tell your whole body to relax and visualise every muscle sinking into the ground, releasing and becoming part of the earth—connected. Bring you awareness back by opening your eyes and moving your fingers and toes. Have a big wake up stretch. Roll over on your side and take a moment to notice how you feel after mindful body relaxation. As with any technique, the more you practice, the easier it will become.

Try going more in-depth; focus on smaller parts of the body while relaxing. Instead of just telling your face to relax, break it down into the parts of the face. Using the same technique as above, start with your brow centre. In your mind, tell the brow centre to relax and visualise the muscles in your brow relaxing. Next, move down to your eyes. In your mind, tell your eyes to relax and visualise the eyes sinking in your sockets, heavy and relaxed. Move to the nose. In your mind, tell that area to relax and visualise the muscles in your nose relaxing. Continue to focus separately on the cheeks, lips, tongue, chin, ears and back of the head. Finally, tell your whole face and head to relax. Visualise every muscle in your face and head melting away; releasing. For the arms, single out the arm pit, upper arm, elbow, lower arm, wrist, palm of the hand, back of the hand and each individual finger. Remember to focus on belly breathing to help keep you calm and relaxed. Repeat this process throughout the whole body. Finally, tell your whole body to relax and visualise every muscle sinking into the ground, releasing and becoming one with the earth.

Remain in this state of stillness and relaxation for as long as you like. When you are ready, slowly bring awareness back into your body and start to move your fingers and toes. Bend your knees and roll over to your left side and just relax there for a few breaths. Come to a sitting position, using your arms to support your body. How do you feel? Take a moment to notice the effects on your mind, body, breathing and awareness.

Recommended Essential Oils

- Arborvitae
- Cedarwood
- Lavender
- Melissa
- Myrrh
- Patchouli
- Roman Chamomile
- Sandalwood
- Ylang Ylang

For topical application, apply 1–3 drops to wrists and/or back of the neck. Inhale directly from the bottle or add 1–3 drops to a diffuser.

These essential oils can be used singularly or in combinations. I have listed some blends that may be helpful but experiment with what combinations work best for you.

Blend 1

- 2 drops arborvitae
- 1 drop cedarwood

Blend 2

- 1 drop ylang ylang
- 1 drop sandalwood
- 1 drop lavender

Blend 3

- 1 drop Roman chamomile
- 1 drop lavender
- 1 drop sandalwood

CHAPTER 17

The Possibilities in Life are Limitless

Life is full of change, challenges and ups and downs, this is a given. If you are expecting life to always be perfect, you are setting yourself up for disappointment and unnecessary suffering. It's about how we handle these situations and what kind of attitude will determine how we cope. The strategies and skills discussed throughout this book will guide you on your journey toward letting go and moving forward. By no means does this book explore *all* the possible options for emotional healing. These are simply strategies that were vital in *my* emotional healing journey. I urge you to explore other possibilities and modalities that could assist you along your personal journey. Colour therapy, body work, light therapy, reflexology, massage or crystals, just to name a few. Make your emotional healing experience all about your individual journey. Stay focused on you, instead of distracting yourself with other people's issues and problems. Be kind to yourself. Emotional healing and finding your true self will take time, with many hiccups along the way. Stick with it. You will backslide into some old behaviours and thinking patterns but this is part of the process; through realising this you will become more aware of your behaviour patterns. This is a positive thing, it shows you are moving forward and facing reality. If at this point you only focus on the fact that you're not perfect, it will be detrimental to your healing journey. Don't beat yourself up for being human.

Life moves in cycles, always flowing and changing. Let go, listen to your intuition and be present in your life. This moment, this hour, this day will never be again. There is no rewind button in life. Start living your life to the fullest, with love and joy in your heart. Someday will always be someday. If you start making little changes every day, you can move mountains. You are good enough, you are strong enough and—YES—you are worth it!

A great way to stay on top of your conscious and subconscious mind is through meditation. Don't underestimate the power of this tool in your arsenal. A calm mind can focus and look past emotional reactions with clear insight. This helps you remain balanced and focused on the present moment instead of living in past regrets or future fears.

In writing this book, I've bared my soul to the world. I have left myself exposed and vulnerable by sharing my personal experiences of abuse, neglect, self-rejection, grief and loss. I have pulled away my mask of false illusion to expose my raw, beautiful self. I have reclaimed my birthright by returning to my maiden name; taking back my power and my identity. My vision is to inspire each of you to share your stories and to be open about your true emotions; it's what defines us as human beings. We all have suppressed, stored emotions that eventually need processing. When we do not process these emotions in a healthy way, they manifest in disease and illness. In the western world, society teaches us to hide behind a mask from a young age. We learn our self-worth and what is acceptable from the world around us and the people in our lives. To top it off, our own body and mind sabotage us by burying these emotions for the purpose of self-preservation.

It is through our connection and awareness of the mind, body and spirit that we can break these cycles and be free. Our experiences of suffering are universal. Let's open up, encourage and support each other as human beings on the same journey of life, instead of hiding, controlling and tearing each other down. We can change the world, we can make a difference; one thought at a time, one action at a time. We can all make a positive difference in our lives and the lives of others. Why not? I challenge you today, not tomorrow, but now—today. Slowly start revealing your true self, warts and all. Only by acknowledging all our behaviours, good and bad, can we move forward. This is the human condition. We all have thoughts of anger, told a lie, judged someone else, gossiped or spoke negatively about another person. It's okay. Through awareness, we can look at these aspects of ourselves and make conscious changes in our lives. There will be people in your life that will react negatively to your healing out of fear. Don't take their fear on as your own, think of it as an opportunity to look deeper into that relationship. How has it affected you? How do you feel after being around that person? What are they really worried about?

Remember, you are never alone; it's okay to reach out for help. Whatever your spiritual belief or situation, there are always options. Sometimes we can't see the forest for the trees and need help seeing the possibilities. It was difficult in the beginning for me to ask for help from anyone. Out of desperation, I reached out and wish I had done it sooner. You will be amazed at the network of individuals out there that can offer you support in different ways.

I also rely on my intuition, which is always present, to guide and comfort me. It provides me with unlimited wisdom, knowledge, support, love, compassion and forgiveness.

You are the only one that can take control of your life and your thoughts. Take responsibility for your actions and live as your true self.

Make a commitment to yourself and open your heart to all the possibilities life has to offer. As you embrace change and personal growth, your world will blossom with love. Above all, be kind to yourself and others; nurture, respect, forgive and show empathy and compassion. We find these things easy to give to others but difficult to accept ourselves. Make a commitment to yourself that you are worth it. The first steps are the most difficult ones to take but you can do it. You are worth it. Believe in yourself and know it's your birth right to live life in joy and abundance.

Stay connected and share your story at
www.trishnashauthor.com

CHAPTER 18

Essential Oils Classification and Emotional Meanings

Arborvitae – *Thuja plicata*

Divinity

- Encourages individuals to not only trust in themselves but also in divine grace
- Releases the need for rigidity and the need to always be in control
- Allows individuals to surrender fear and to instead trust in the flow of life
- Brings comfort that divine grace is ever-present
- Assists the soul in following a greater path

Basil – *Ocimum basilicum*

Renewing

- Emotionally supports individuals who feel overwhelmed and unable to cope with the stress of life
- Assists with feelings of exhaustion, chronic fatigue or low energy
- Assists individuals recovering from addiction
- Comforts individuals in states of nervousness, depression or anxiety

Bergamot – *Citrus bergamia*
Accepting one's self
- Emotionally supports individuals to overcome feelings of low self-esteem or self-judgement
- Encourages unconditional self-love
- Promotes confidence and feelings of abundance
- Helps alleviate feelings of depression, addiction and anxiety

Birch – *Betula lenta*
Supports
- Helps individuals who feel unsupported
- Provides courage, helping individuals to move forward with strength
- Encourages feelings of belonging and connection to the world
- Addresses generational patterns of rejection
- Balances and supports

Black Pepper – *Piper nigrum*
Unmasking
- Assists individuals to reveal their true self by peeling back the false layers
- Reveals repressed, buried feelings of judgement
- Allows individuals to move forward by honestly acknowledging the reasons behind addictive, compulsive behaviours
- Helps facilitate health boundaries

Cardamom – *Elettaria cardamomum*
Objectivity
- Assists individuals who become easily frustrated and fly off the handle in anger and frustration
- Brings focus to the mind, enabling distorted views to become clear

- Encourages balance in the midst of extreme anger, allowing the individual to process their emotions in a health way

Cassia – *Cinnamomum cassia*
Self-reassurance
- Assists individuals who lack confidence and are hindered by shyness and feelings of worthlessness
- Restores confidence and releases fears
- Assists with providing courage to stop individuals from hiding out of embarrassment and insecurity
- Helps to discover hidden talents and gifts, enabling individuals to live out of their true self

Cedarwood – *Juniperus virginiana*
Connection to community
- Creates feelings of connection with community and positive bonds within social groups
- Allows the heart to open, accepting love and support from others in the community
- Helps reconnect individuals with roots and family
- Leaves individuals feeling support and balanced

Cilantro – *Coriandrum sativum* (leaf)
Letting go of control
- Encourages individuals to release toxic, negative feelings that make them feel trapped
- Releases the need to obsessively control self, others and the environment
- Allows emotional cleansing and frees the soul

Cinnamon Bark – *Cinnamomum zeylanicum*
Sexual balance
- Encourages individuals to accept their sexuality and body, freeing them from the need to control
- Helps release feelings of fear and rejection stemming from sexual insecurities
- Stimulates sexual desire and the need for intimacy and vulnerability in relationships
- Balances repressed sexuality or over sexuality

Clary Sage – *Salvia sclarea*
Vision and clarity
- Opens the door to the truth by releasing false life scripts
- Helps individuals to broaden and open their mind
- Stimulates new ideas, creativity, imagination and clarity
- Promotes individuals to see a new perspective
- Connects individuals with their spiritual gifts and talents

Clove Bud – *Eugenia caryophyllata*
Personal boundaries
- Frees individuals from the victim mentality by igniting their personal power
- Assists individuals to reclaim their life and let go of destructive behaviours, patterns and self-sabotage
- Uplifts the soul to release past abuse and trauma by living out of true self
- Encourages healthy boundaries
- Supports individuals to stand up for themselves and their beliefs

Coriander – *Coriandrum Sativum* (seed)
Loyalty to self
- Helps individuals who always serve others while neglecting their own needs
- Promotes individuals to show loyalty and honour to themselves instead of conforming to the views of others
- Connects individuals to their spirituality
- Helps individuals to realise that there are many ways to do and see things

Cypress – *Cupressus sempervirens*
Circulation and flow
- Promotes balance and flexibility
- Encourages individuals to let go of control and reject behaviours that keep them stuck and inflexible
- Helps individuals to release the need for perfectionism and let go of the past to move forward with ease
- Helps release fear and anxiety about the future

Eucalyptus – *Eucalyptus radiata*
Health and wellness
- Supports individuals stuck in a perpetual loop of illness by releasing their attachment and desire to escape life
- Challenges life scripts and fear of responsibility
- Addresses feelings of despair and defeat in life
- Promotes wholeness and healing
- Teaches individuals to take responsibility for their own health

Fennel – *Foeniculum vulgare (sweet)*
Ownership and responsibility
- Encourages individuals to take responsibility for their life
- Teaches individuals that no challenge is too big to handle
- Sheds light on a weakened sense of true self
- Allows individuals to move beyond fear
- Reconnects individuals to ideas of nurturing their bodies on a spiritual and physical level
- Ignites passion for life, dulling the need to numb and disconnect

Frankincense – Boswellia frereana
Truthfulness
- Reveals false truths, negativity and self-deception
- Sheds light on notions of the true self
- Supports individuals to feel loved by life and the divine
- Helps individuals to release toxic energies, allowing them to live out of light and their spiritual gifts
- Like a loving father, Frankincense protects
- Releases individuals from their false mask by nurturing and reconnecting with the divine self
- Dispels feelings of abandonment, loneliness, grief and loss
- Supports the inner child

Geranium – *Pelargonium graveolens*
Trust and love
- Geranium is a powerful emotional healer as it gently encourages individuals to face their pain and move forward with forgiveness
- Encourages feelings of trust and love for others
- Promotes connection to one's mother
- Reconnects individuals to the goodness in the world

- Softens the most hardened heart, allowing love and acceptance
- Cradles individuals during grief, loss and heartbreak

Ginger – *Zingiber officinate*
Empowering
- Addresses life scripts relating to self-esteem and victim mentality, enabling individuals to take back their personal power
- Ignites passion and full participation in life
- Helps individuals move forward by taking responsibility for their self and their life
- Empowers individuals to take charge of life with determination and integrity
- Holds individuals accountable for actions
- Assists individuals to live in the present moment

Grapefruit – *Citrus paradisi (peel)*
Respecting the physical body
- Supports individuals to honour, respect and appreciate their physical body without judgement
- Releases anxiety over body image
- Transforms self-hatred to self-love
- Assists in breaking unhealthy patterns of food addiction, strict dieting or eating disorders
- Allows individuals to break free and take ownership of their emotions

Helichrysum – *Helichrysum italicum*
Releasing pain
- Releases pain
- Assists in healing the wounded
- Provides strength in times of trauma, loss, addiction or abuse

- Offers resilience and hope
- Promotes gratitude
- Guides individuals to find the silver lining in their situation and encouragement to live life
- Opens the heart to heal emotional wounds

Jasmine – *Jasminum officinale*
Reveals the deepest layers of the soul

- Allows individuals to look inward, past all the layers of illusion and life scripts
- Reconnects individuals to their spiritual self, allowing them to live out of their true self in love and light
- Supports individuals to realise their spiritual gift and connection to universal energy

Juniper Berry – *Juniperus communis*
Darkness of the night

- Assists individuals to look within, past the fear, to discover their true self buried in the darkness
- Encourages individuals to face their fears with honesty instead of hiding in the shadows
- Offers individuals an opportunity to process unresolved fears by bring them to the light
- Restores the balance between opposing forces of light and dark
- Dispels fears of the night
- Taps into the subconscious mind and the dream world

Lavender – *Lavandula angustifolia*
Communicating

- Addresses fears of speaking up for one's self
- Offers courage to verbally express thoughts and emotions

- Supports honesty and the ability to look inward for expression of true self
- Releases anxiety
- Promotes self-acceptance by expressing true feeling and ideas without fear of rejection
- Releases repressed memories

Lemon – *Citrus limon*
Clarity and focus
- Assists with concentration and clears the mind of confusion
- Brings clarity in order to forgive and release self-judgement
- Allows individuals to live life with happiness and joy
- Lifts depressive states and energies in the mind and body
- Restores confidence
- Aids in learning disorders
- Provides a sense of abundance in life

Lemongrass – *Cymbopogon flexuosus*
Cleansing negative energies
- Releases toxic negative energies, breathing new life back into an individual
- Helps individuals to move forward from the past and commit to emotional healing
- Peels back the darkness to reveal life scripts and negativity caused by despair and anxiety
- Assists individuals to let go of excessive material possessions

Lime – *Citrus aurantifolia*
Lust for life
- Lifts the soul
- Encourages individuals to live with gratitude and joy

- Encourages hope and a zest for life
- Releases depression and suicidal tendencies
- Clears the heart, opening it up to allow love, light and happiness to abundantly flow
- Promotes balance between the intellectual mind and the working of the heart

Marjoram – *Origanum majorana*
Connecting
- Marjoram helps individuals to release fear and form close, meaningful relationships with others
- Encourages trust and forgiveness from past experiences
- Connects individuals to embrace their emotions and fears of rejection, allowing them to move forward out of love
- Promotes individuals to honestly look inward to address self-sabotaging tendencies used as a protection from being hurt again

Melaleuca – *Melaleuca alternifolia*
Energetic boundaries
- Guards against parasitic relationships and clears toxic, negative energies
- Encourages strong boundaries and empowers individuals to respect themselves
- Addresses the subconscious need that individuals have to allow co-dependent relationship in their lives
- Assist individuals with the courage to stand up for themselves

Melissa – *Melissa officinalis* (lemon balm)
Enlightens
- Reconnects individuals with the truth
- Awakens the soul by shining light and life on the true self

- Uplifts the darkened, depressed individuals, lightening the load of life
- Provides spiritual guidance and a reconnection to true self
- Assists in shedding thoughts of suicide
- Turns feeling of being overwhelmed into balance and harmony
- Releases past trauma or abuse

Myrrh – *Commiphora myrrha*
Mother Nature
- Nurtures the soul and reconnects it to Mother Earth
- Rekindles the relationship with maternal mother where disharmony is present
- Encourages reattachment by releasing feelings of abandonment, childhood trauma and malnourishment
- Assists individuals to feel safe and secure in the world
- Facilitates forgiveness of others and an openness to trust again

Orange – *Citrus sinensis* (Peel)
Abundance in all things
- Assists individuals to live life with abundance and happiness
- Promotes creativity, joy and generosity to others
- Dispels depressive states by invigorating the mind and body
- Addresses the need individuals have to overwork and take life too seriously
- Encourages individuals to let go of material possession and flow through life with flexibility

Oregano – *Origanum vulgare*
Detachment
- Removes and clears negative energies, allowing individuals to break negative attachments

- Opens one's eyes to other points of view
- Allows individuals to detach from rigid beliefs, over attachment to their job, material possessions and relationships that hinder their true self
- Releases the need to always be right, which hinders the possibilities in life

Patchouli – *Pogostemom cablin*
Physically present
- Helps individuals to reconnect with their spiritual self
- Balances spiritual awareness and escapism from physical body
- Assists individuals to reconnect with their body, letting go of judgement and shame
- Relaxes and builds confidence by releasing negative distorted body image
- Reconnects mind and body from experiences of sexual abuse

Peppermint – *Mentha piperita*
Lifts and lightens the heart
- Assists in relieving fear and living life with joy
- Uplifts the heart and soul, allowing individuals to float through life
- Promotes happiness and relieves deep depression
- Supports in times of extreme emotional pain
- Facilitates emotional growth
- Teaches individuals to look at life through optimistic eyes

Roman Chamomile – *Anthemis nobilis*
Spiritual journey
- Reduces feeling of anxiety
- Assists individuals to discover their true purpose and meaning in life

- Supports the letting go of mundane, meaningless activities to make way for productive ones
- Allows individuals to live their true self
- Gives purpose
- Balances spiritual energies to encourage growth
- Releases frustration and calms the mind

Rose – *Rosa damascena*
Universal love
- Heals the heart and opens the doors for self-love
- Reconnects individuals with their inner-child
- Dispels feelings of loneliness
- Assists in establishing a connection to others and the universe through unconditional love
- Restores belief in humanity
- Reaffirms the never-changing, always-present divine guidance and unconditional love
- Opens the heart to allow love to easily flow to every part of the soul

Rosemary – *Rosmarinus officinalis*
Information and transition
- Provides focus and clarity to look beyond the limited understanding of the mind
- Assists individuals to transcend to a higher level of knowledge and wisdom to expand consciousness
- Supports individuals during transitions and changes in life
- Unlocks a higher self-intelligence, enabling a greater understanding and confidence when faced with new situations in life

Sandalwood, Hawaiian – *Santalum paniculatum*
Spirituality
- Relaxes and calms anxiety
- Reconnects individuals with their spiritual self and the divine
- Supports in re-evaluating what is important in life and realigning spiritual beliefs
- Quiets the body, mind and soul to connect with the divine through mediation or prayer
- Promotes feeling of wholeness by raising the conscious mind

Spearmint – *Mentha spicata*
Open and releasing emotional blockages
- Releases repressed memories of abuse, trauma, grief and loss
- Allows individuals to forgive and move forward in life
- Supports individuals to accept the truth and know that nothing is too hard to handle
- Encourages connection to self and the notion that individuals are never alone
- Assists individuals to live life in abundance and courage

Tangerine – *Citrus reticulata*
Joy and self-expression
- Supports individuals to live life with joy and playfulness
- Uplifts the downtrodden heart out of depression and into the light
- Promotes creativity and relaxes unrealistic standards of self
- Encourages flexibility and opens a heavy heart to allow life to spontaneously flow
- Releases the need to self-sabotage and overburden life with responsibility

Thyme – *Thymus vulgaris*
Letting go and forgiveness
- Releases deep, stagnant emotions that keeps individuals tied to bitterness and resentment
- Supports in opening the heart to forgiveness of self and others
- Allows individuals to release feeling of anger, hate and rage
- Assists in embracing the future to free individuals from the chains of emotional bondage

Vetiver – *Vetiveria zizanioides*
Grounding and balancing
- Assists individuals to become grounded in life
- Supports individuals when looking inward to reconnect with thoughts and feelings on a generational level
- Assists with being in the present moment, fully descending into the light and discovering the true self
- Reduces stress and anxiety
- Balances a scattered mind

White Fir – *Abies alba*
Healing generational wounds
- Shines a light on hidden, negative generational patterns like pride, hate, abuse, anger and addiction
- Allows individuals to break free from destructive family patterns
- Supports the release of burdens placed on individuals through hereditary and generational constraints, allowing them to be set free
- Assists to ground the true self

Wintergreen – *Gaultheria procumbens*
Surrendering
- Assists individuals to let go of the past
- Releases the need for control
- Supports letting go of the weight of the world by releasing obsessive self-reliance
- Replaces the need to always be right
- Promotes a connection with the divine
- Comforts individuals with the fact that they are not alone

Ylang Ylang – *Cananga odorata*
True self and inner child
- Re-establishes a connection to the inner self and childlike nature of a pure heart
- Releases emotional trauma, grief and loss
- Supports individuals in respecting the emotional healing power of the heart
- Calms anxiety and relieves stress
- Enables individuals to live with joy and love

Essential Oils Safety Reference Chart

Essential Oil Name	Topical			Aromatic		
	Adult	Pregnant	Child	Adult	Pregnant	Child
Arborvitae *Thuja plicata*	N	S	S	N	S	N
Basil *Ocimum basilicum*	N	D	S	N	S	N
Bergamot *Citrus bergamia* **	N	N	S	N	N	N
Birch *Betula lenta*	N	X	S	N	X	N
Black Pepper *Piper nigrum*	S	S	D	S	S	S
Cardamom *Elettaria cardamomum*	N	N	N	N	N	N
Cassia *Cinnamomum cassia*	D	X	D	S	S	S
Cedarwood *Juniperus virginiana*	N	S	S	N	S	N
Cilantro *Coriandrum sativum* (leaf)	N	N	S	N	N	N
Cinnamon Bark *Cinnamomum zeylanicum*	D	X	D	S	S	S
Clary Sage *Salvia sclarea*	N	D	N	N	S	N
Clove Bud *Eugenia caryophyllata*	S	S	D	S	S	S
Coriander *Coriandrum Sativum* (seed)	N	N	N	N	N	N
Cypress *Cupressus sempervirens*	N	S	N	N	N	N
Eucalyptus *Eucalyptus radiata*	N	N	S	N	N	N
Fennel *Foeniculum vulgare* (sweet)	N	D	S	N	S	N
Frankincense *Boswellia frereana*	N	N	N	N	N	N

Essential Oils Safety Reference Chart

Essential Oil Name	Topical			Aromatic		
	Adult	Pregnant	Child	Adult	Pregnant	Child
Geranium *Pelargonium graveolens*	N	N	S	N	N	N
Ginger *Zingiber officinate* *	N	N	S	N	N	N
Grapefruit *Citrus paradisi* (peel)	N	N	N	N	N	N
Helichrysum *Helichrysum italicum*	N	X	N	N	X	N
Jasmine *Jasminum officinale*	N	X	S	N	X	N
Juniper Berry *Juniperus communis*	N	S	N	N	S	N
Lavender *Lavandula angustifolia*	N	N	N	N	N	N
Lemon *Citrus limon* *	N	N	N	N	N	N
Lemongrass *Cymbopogon flexuosus*	N	S	S	N	S	N
Lime *Citrus aurantifolia* *	N	N	N	N	N	N
Marjoram *Origanum majorana*	N	D	S	N	S	N
Melaleuca *Melaleuca alternifolia*	N	N	N	N	N	N
Melissa *Melissa officinalis* (lemon balm)	N	N	N	N	N	N
Myrrh *Commiphora myrrha*	N	S	N	N	S	N
Orange *Citrus sinensis* (Peel) *	N	N	N	N	N	N
Oregano *Origanum vulgare*	D	D	D	N	S	N

Patchouli *Pogostemom cablin*	N	N	N	N	N	N
Peppermint *Mentha piperita*	S	S	N	S	S	N
Roman Chamomile *Anthemis nobilis*	N	N	N	S	N	N
Rose *Rosa damascena*	N	S	N	N	N	N
Rosemary *Rosmarinus officinalis*	N	X	N	X	X	N
Sandalwood, Hawaiian *Santalum paniculatum*	N	N	N	N	N	N
Spearmint *Mentha spicata*	S	S	N	S	S	N
Tangerine *Citrus reticulata* **	N	S	N	S	N	N
Thyme *Thymus vulgaris*	D	X	N	D	X	S
Vetiver *Vetiveria zizanioides*	N	S	N	N	S	N
White Fir *Abies alba*	N	N	N	S	N	N
Wintergreen *Gaultheria procumbens*	N	X	N	S	X	N
Ylang Ylang *Cananga odorata*	N	N	N	S	N	N

Key

Skin Sensitivity:
N – Neat, no dilution.
S – Moderate dilution.
D – Heavy dilution.
X – Not recommended for usage.

Sun Sensitivity:
* – Avoid sunlight for up to 3 hours after topical usage.
** – Avoid sunlight for up to 12–24 hours after topical usage.

Consult with a physician if taking prescription medications or pregnant.

References

Aroma Tools Modern Essentials, A Contemporary Guide to the Therapeutic Use of Essential Oils, fifth edition. 2014.

Bachmann, Margrit, Introducing Aromatherapy. 1996.

Battaglia, Salvatore, The Enchanting Art of Aromatherapy. 1988.

Bottom Line Books, The World's Greatest Treasury of Health Secrets. 2005.

Bowles, E. Joy, The A to Z of Essential Oils, What They Are, Where They Come From, How They Work. 2003.

Conny, Beth Mende, Believe in Yourself, A Woman's Journey. 1994.

Downes, Karen and White, Judith Aromatherapy for Scentual Awareness, second edition. 1992.

Enlighten Alternative Healing, LLC Emotions & Essential Oils, A Modern Resource for Healing, second edition. 2013.

Evans, Mark K., Mind Body Spirt, A Practical Guide to Natural Therapies for Healthiness and Well Being.

Greer, Allica, Meditation is Powerful, The Power of Thought to Change Your Life. 2001.

Grace, Nicola, Freedom from Sexual Abuse. 1993.

Hansard, Christopher, The Tibetan art of Living, Wise Body, Wise Mind, Wise Life. 2001.

Hay, Louise L., Heal Your Body, The Mental Causes for Physical Illness and the Metaphysical Way to Overcome Them. 1982.

Hicks, Ester and Jerry, Ask And It Is Given, Learning to Manifest Your Desires.

James, R L., Essentials of the Earth, An Encyclopedia of Oils, Blends and Applications, third edition. 2013.

Lhundrup, Venerable Thubten, Practical Meditation with Buddhist Principles. 2006.

McGilvery, Carole; Reed, Jimi, The Essential Aromatherapy Book, A Comprehensive Guide to Using Essential Oils for Health, Relaxation and Pleasure. 1995.

Miller, Light ND; Miller, Bryan DC, Ayurveda & Aromatherapy, The Earth Essential Guide to Ancient Wisdom and Modern Healing.

Ricard, Mattieu, Why Meditate? Working With Thoughts and Emotions. 2008.

Ryman, Daniele, The Aromatherapy Handbook, The Secret Healing Power of Essential Oils. 1984.

Stenton, Deborah, The Good, The Bad, The Relationship. 2016.

Worwood, Valerie Ann, The Fragrant Heavens, The Spiritual Dimension of Fragrance and Aromatherapy. 1999.

About the Author

American-born author Trish Nash has a Bachelor of Arts in Psychology and Business Communication from Bowling Green State University. A certified Clinical Master Aromatherapist and reiki and thetahealing practitioner, Trish also holds certificates in small business management, aged care, and children's services.

Trish is a published author, mentor, public speaker, life coach, and doTERRA wellness advocate. She has over 18 years' experience as a practitioner, program director, educator, and business owner in the fields of aromatherapy, natural healing, disabilities, child care, and aged care.

Trish passionately believes in giving back to the community by volunteering for Days for Girls, Education Queensland, and Scenic Rim Regional Council; offering aromatherapy treatments at Churches of Christ Care; and acting as board member of the Local Community Garden.

On her personal journey of emotional healing, Trish fell in love with doTERRA Essential Oils, which gave birth to this book, *Emotional Healing with Essential Oils*. Here, her passion for the benefits of essential oils harmonically aligns with her desire for helping others on their own emotional, physical, and spiritual healing journeys.